Contents

Overview of the Civil Partnerships Act 2004

Overview of the Act

This brief introduction provides an overview of the Civil Partnerships Act 2004. It is intended to provide a back ground to the more detailed information provided within the body of the text contained in this book. The information has been updated to 2010.

The book does not cover Scotland or Northern Ireland, which are contained in Parts 3 and 4 to the Act, although there are references to both countries throughout. The Act is similar throughout the United Kingdom, but there are differences to take into account different legal systems. For further details on the Act as it applies in Scotland and Northern Ireland you should go to the government website which displays the Act in its entirety: www. legislation.gov.uk.

Appendix one outlines various statistics concerning formation of civil partnerships and also dissolutions since the Act was implemented in 2005. The statistics cover the period 2005-2009.

Civil Partnerships

Part 1 of the Civil Partnerships Act 2004 introduces and defines a civil partnership. A Civil partnership is a new legal relationship, which can be registered by two people of the same sex. Same sex couples within a civil partnership can obtain legal recognition for their relationship and can obtain the same benefits generally as married couples.

The Civil Partnerships Act came into force on 5th December 2005. The first civil partnerships registered in England and Wales took place on 21st December 2005. Civil partners will be treated the same as married couples in many areas, including:

- Tax, including inheritance tax
- Employment benefits
- Most state and occupational pension benefits
- Income related benefits, tax credits and child support
- Maintenance for partner and children
- Ability to apply for parental responsibility for a child
- Inheritance of a tenancy agreement
- Recognition under intestacy rules
- Access to fatal accidents compensation

- Protection from domestic violence
- Recognition for immigration and nationality purposes

The registration of a civil partnership

Part 2, Chapter 1, of the Act introduces the registration process. Two people may register a civil partnership provided they are of the same sex, not already in a civil partnership or legally married, not closely related and both over 16 although consent of a parent or guardian must be obtained if either of them are under 18.

Registering a civil partnership is a secular procedure and is carried out by the registration service, which is responsible for the registration of births, deaths and marriages. A civil partnership registration is carried out under what is termed a standard procedure, which can be varied to take into account housebound people or people who are ill and are not expected to recover.

The standard procedure for registering a civil partnership

A couple wishing to register a civil partnership just have to decide the date they want to register and where they want the registration to take place. The formal process for registering consists of two main stages-the giving of a notice of intention to register and then the registration of the civil partnership itself.

The first stage, the giving of notice is a legal requirement and both partners have to do this at a register office in the area of a local authority where they live, even if they intend to register elsewhere. The notice contains the names, age, marital or civil partnership status, address, occupation, nationality and intended venue for the civil partnership. It is a criminal offence to give false information. If one of the partners is a non-EAA citizen and subject to immigration controls (see later) there are additional requirements to be fulfilled. Once the notice has been given it is displayed at the relevant register office for 15 days. This provides an opportunity for objections to be made. The civil partnership cannot be registered until after 15 clear days have elapsed from the date of the second person gives notice.

Each partner needs to give notice in the area that they have lived for at least seven days. If the couple live in different areas then each will post a notice in their own relevant area. When giving notice they will be asked where they wish the civil partnership to take place.

Residency requirements for a civil partnerships

A couple can register a civil partnership in England and Wales as long as they have both lived in a registration district in England and Wales for at least seven days immediately before giving notice. If one person lives in Scotland and the other lives in England or Wales, the person living in Scotland may give notice there. Officers, sailors or marines on board a Royal Navy ship at sea can give notice to the captain or other commanding officer, providing they are going to register with someone who is resident in England and Wales. Service personnel based outside England and Wales have to fulfil the above residence requirements.

Documentary evidence of name, age and nationality will need to be shown. Passports and birth certificates are the main documents required. Proof of address will be required. If either partner has been married or in a civil partnership before, then evidence of divorce or dissolution will be required. If either partner is subject to immigration control a document showing entry clearance granted to form a civil partnership will need to be shown, along with a home office certificate of approval and indefinite leave to remain in the UK.

Civil partnership registration

A civil partnership registration can take place in any register office in England and Wales or at any venue that has been approved to hold a civil partnership. Approved premises include stately homes and other prestigious buildings including hotels and restaurants. From 5th December 2005, any venue that has approval for civil marriage will automatically be approved for civil partnerships. A civil partnership cannot be registered on a religious premises. A civil partnership can only be registered between the hours of 8am to 6pm unless one person is seriously ill and is not expected to recover.

A civil partnership is legally registered once the couple have signed the legal document, known as a civil partnership schedule, in the presence of a registrar and two witnesses. On the day, two witnesses will be required. If they wish to do so, the couple will be able to speak to each other the words contained in the schedule:

' I declare that I know of no legal reason why we may not register as each other's civil partner. I understand that on signing this document we will be forming a civil partnership with each other'

No religious service may take place, as the process of forming a civil partnership is entirely secular. A ceremony can be arranged to accompany the actual registration. This ceremony can take place at any venue as long as it is approved.

Costs of registering a civil partnership

The costs here are applicable to 2010/11. Like all other costs they will change from year to year and the current costs should always be ascertained by contacting your local register office.

The current costs are as follows:

- Giving notice of intention to register   £33.50
- Registration at Register Office   £40

Registration at an approved premises-in this case the cost for attendance by a civil partnership registrar is set by the registration authority in question. A further charge may also be made by the owner for use of the building,

- Cost of civil partnership certificate on the day of registration £3.50
- Further copies of the civil partnership certificate £7

The General Register Office website www.grogo.uk has a search facility if you need to find a local register office or an office any where in the UK.

Changing names

After registering a civil partnership, one partner might want to change their surname to that of their partner. Government departments and agencies will accept civil partnership certificates as evidence for changing surnames. Other private institutions may want a different form of evidence. It is up to the individual to check with the various organisations if they wish to change their surname.

Special circumstances

Variations to the standard procedure can be made in certain circumstances. If a partner is seriously ill and is not expected to recover then a civil partnership can be registered at any time. The 15-day waiting period will not apply. A certificate will need to be provided from a doctor stating that a person is not expected to recover and cannot be moved to a place where civil partnerships take place and that they understand the nature and purpose of signing the Registrar Generals licence.

Housebound people

If one partner is housebound there are special procedures to allow them to register a civil partnership at home. A statement has to be signed, made by a doctor, confirming that this is the case and that the condition is likely to continue for the next three months. The statement must have been made no more than 14 days before notice being given and must be made on a standard form provided by the register office. The normal 15-day period will apply between giving notice and the civil partnership registration.

Detained people

There are special procedures to allow a couple to register a civil partnership at a place where one of them is detained in a hospital or prison. The couple has to provide a statement, made by the prison governor or responsible person confirming that the place where a person is detained can be named in the notice of proposed civil partnership as the place where the registration is to take place. This statement must have been made no more than 21 days prior to notice being given. The normal 15 day waiting period applies.

Gender change

The Gender Recognition Act 2004 enables transsexual people to change their legal gender by obtaining a full Gender Recognition Certificate. Where a transsexual person is married, they cannot obtain a full Gender Recognition Certificate without first ending their existing marriage. However, if they and their former spouse then wish to form a civil partnership with one another without delay, they can do so as soon as the full Gender Recognition Certificate has been issued. In those circumstances, they give notice and register on the same day. More information is available about the process of changing gender on www.grp.gro.uk

Immigration requirements for people subject to immigration controls

The civil partnerships provisions for people subject to immigration control are exactly the same as those in place for marriage. These apply if one partner is a non-EAA (European Immigration Area) citizen and is subject to immigration control, for example in the UK on a visa.

People subject to immigration control who want to give notice of a civil partnership need to do so at a register office designated for this purpose. They are required to produce one of the following as part of that notice:

- entry clearance granted to form a civil partnership
- A Home Office certificate of approval
- Indefinite leave to remain in the UK.

Registrars are required to report any civil partnerships to the immigration service if they have any suspicions.

Application for leave to remain

Civil partners of British citizens and people settled here can apply for an initial period of two years leave to remain in the UK. If they are still together at the end of that period they can apply for indefinite leave to remain.

Work permit holders and students

Civil partners of people with temporary leave to remain in the UK, such as students and work permit holders, can apply for leave along with their civil partners.

A list of Register Offices for people subject to immigration control, can be found at www.ind.homeoffice.gov.uk

Civil partnership registration for two non-EAA citizens

Two non-EAA citizens can register a civil partnership together in the UK as long as they have entry clearance for the purpose of doing so and have resided in the registration district for at least seven days before giving notice. Registering a civil partnership doesn't affect their immigration status.

Registering civil partnerships abroad

If couples wish to register a civil partnership abroad they should contact the Embassy or High Commission in the country concerned. Couples may be asked to obtain a certificate of no impediment.

It may be possible for couples to register at a UK consulate in another country if one of them is a UK national. However, UK consulates will not register civil partnerships if the host country objects or if civil unions or same sex marriage is available in that country.

Armed Forces

Members of the Armed Forces can register civil partnerships overseas in those areas where a Servicing Registering Officer is able to offer this service.

Overseas relationships

It may be the case that a couple has formed a civil union, registered partnership, domestic partnership or same-sex marriage abroad. Couples in those kind of relationships can automatically be recognised in the UK as civil partners without having to register again provided conditions set out in sections 212 to 218 of the Civil Partnership Act are met.

The legislation defines an overseas relationship that can be treated as a civil partnership in the UK as one that is either specified in Schedule 20 to the Civil Partnership Act or one which meets general conditions in the Act and certain other conditions. Schedule 20 of the Act lists countries and relationships that are recognised. Countries listed in the Act are:

- Andorra
- Australia: Tasmania
- Belgium
- Canada-Novia Scotia and Quebec
- Denmark (including Greenland)
- Finland
- France
- Germany
- Iceland
- Luxembourg
- Netherlands
- New Zealand
- Norway
- Spain
- Sweden
- USA-Vermont-Connecticut-Maine-Massachusetts-New Jersey.

The above are correct as at 2011 but should be checked as they are subject to change.

A couple who have formed a relationship recognised in one of those countries can be recognised in the UK as civil partners if they are of the same sex, the relationship has been registered with a responsible body in that country, the couple were eligible to enter into a civil relationship in that country and all procedural requirements have been fulfilled.

For foreign relationships in countries not listed in Schedule 20 a couple who have formed a relationship can still be recognised as civil partners if the foreign relationship meets the general conditions set out in the Civil Partnerships Act.

To find out which foreign relationships are contained within Schedule 20, which is revised periodically, go to www.equalities.gov.uk

Dissolution of relationships formed abroad

Where a couple have formed an overseas relationship and that relationship is treated as a civil partnership in the UK, they may be able to obtain a dissolution, annulment or legal separation here. Legal advice should be sought in this matter.

Family relationships

The law now recognises the role of both civil partners in respect of a child living in their household.

Adoption

Under the Adoption and Children Act 2002, which came into force on 30th December 2005, civil partners may apply jointly to adopt a child.

Parental responsibility

Under the Adoption and Children Act 2002, a person will also be able to acquire parental responsibility for the child of their civil partner. They can do this with the agreement of their civil partner. If the childs other parent also has parental responsibility, both parents must agree. Parental responsibility can also be acquired on application to the court. Civil partners will have a duty to provide maintenance for each other and any children of the civil partnership.

Social security, tax credits and child support

Entering into a civil partnership will affect entitlements to the benefits and tax credits a person may be receiving. From 5th December 2005, the income of a civil partner has been taken into account when calculating entitlement to income related benefits. These benefits include income support, income based job seekers allowance, pension credit, housing benefit and council tax benefit.

For a list of benefits and other advice contact the Benefit Enquiry Line on 0800 882200.

Tax credits

From 5th December the income of a civil partner has been taken into account when calculating entitlement to child and working tax credits. The Tax Credit Line on 0904 169 0072 can offer further advice.

Child support

From 5th December 2005, civil partners who are parents will be treated in the same way as married partners for child support. Also, parents who are living with a same sex partner even where they have not formed a civil partnership will be treated in the same way as parents who live together with an opposite sex partner but who are not married.

For further information contact the Child Support Agency on 08457 133133.

Pensions

Survivor benefits in occupational and personal pension schemes. Surviving civil partners will be entitled to a pension based on accrued pension right. New rules for civil partners mean that a surviving partner will benefit from a survivors pension based on the contracted out pension rights accrued by their deceased partner from 1988 to the date of retirement or death if this occurs before retirement. This new rule applies to all contracted out private pension schemes.

State pensions

From 5th December 2005, civil partners have enjoyed most of the same state pension rights as husbands and they will treated the same as husbands and wives after 2010 when the treatment of men and women will be equalised. For more information concerning pensions contact the Pension Service on 0845 6060625.

Tax

From 5th December 2005, civil partners have been treated the same as married couples for tax purposes. Information is available from a local tax office and the HMRC website www.hmrc.gov.uk

Employment rights

Employers are required to treat both married partners and civil partners in the same way. The Employment Equality (Sexual Orientation) Regulations 2003 have been amended to ensure that civil partners receive the same treatment and can bring a claim for sexual orientation discrimination if this is not the case. Other areas where changes are made include flexible working, where a civil partner of a child under six or disabled child under 18 will be able to take advantage of flexible working arrangements. Paternity and adoption leave will now be the right of civil partners More information on paternity and adoption leave and pay can be found on www.dti.gov.uk/workingparents.

Wills

Like all people, couples or not, making a will is the most sensible way of ensuring equitable disposal of your assets in accordance with your wishes. The most valuable asset is usually a home and this will automatically vest in a civil partner after death of the other partner, whether or not a will expressly states this. All other property belonging to one of the civil partners will be disposed of according to the will.

If a person has a will and then registers a civil partnership it will be revoked automatically unless it expressly states otherwise.

If a person dies without making a will there are special legal rules which determine how the estate of the deceased should be shared amongst that persons relatives. Under the new law, if a civil partner dies intestate then his or her civil partner can receive a maximum of £200,000 from the estate and a half share of the amount that is left. If the deceased had children then the amount which the surviving civil partner automatically receives is £125,000 and a half share of the rest.

An application to the court can be made if a surviving civil partner feels that the will doesn't make adequate provision for them.

Life assurance

Civil partners can hold life insurance on their partner's life on the same basis as a married person. In the event of an accident caused by negligence of another then the civil partner can claim compensation and can claim bereavement damages, currently £10,000. Similarly, someone living with the deceased as though they had been in a civil partnership for two years prior to date of death will also be entitled to claim compensation as a dependant.

Tenancy rights

The general effect of the Civil Partnerships Act has been to give the same rights to civil partners as married couples. The Act also equalises the rights of same sex couples who are living together as if they were civil partners and their families with those of unmarried opposite sex couples.

Private sector tenants

The same sex partner of an assured tenant or assured shorthold tenant will have the same rights of succession to a tenancy as those tenants of local authority or registered social landlords. For further information on housing and tenancies visit www.communities.gov.uk

Dissolution of a civil partnership

Part 2, Chapter 2 contains the provisions for the dissolution of a civil partnership. A civil partnership ends only on the death of one of the civil partners, or on the dissolution of the partnership or a nullity odder or a presumption of death order by the court.

The usual route is for one of the partners to seek a dissolution order to terminate the civil partnership. Other options are available. If one party, for example, did not validly consent as a result of duress, mistake or unsoundness of mind, then a nullity order may be sought from the court, or if both civil partners do not wish to terminate the partnership one of them may ask the court for a separation order.

The dissolution process

Whoever decides to end the civil partnership should seek legal advice. The case will usually be dealt with by a civil partnership proceedings county court, although complex cases will be referred to the high court.

To end a civil partnership the applicant (petitioner) must prove to the court that the civil partnership has irretrievably broken down. Proof of an irretrievable breakdown is based on the following:

- Unreasonable behaviour by both or other civil partner
- Separation for two years with the consent of the other civil partner
- Separation for five years without the consent of the other civil partner
- If the other civil partner has deserted the applicant for a period of two years or more.

Nullity

In exceptional circumstances one party to a civil partnership may decide to seek a court order (a 'Nullity' order) to annul the civil partnership.

Separation

The grounds on which a separation order may be sought are exactly the same as those for a dissolution order. The end result is different, as a person whose civil partnership has been dissolved is free to marry or form a new partnership whereas a person who has separated remains a civil partner.

Property and financial arrangements

Part 2 Chapter 3 deals with property and financial relationships. If a civil partnership is ending or if the couple are separating, they will need to decide what happens to any property belonging to them. If they agree on a division they can ask the court to approve the agreement. If they cannot agree they can ask the court to decide. The court has power to make a range of orders in relation to property and other assets including income:

- The court can make an order that one civil partner pay maintenance to the other either for the benefit of the civil partner or for the benefit of any children of the relationship. These orders are known as financial provision orders.
- The court can make an order which will adjust the property rights of the civil partners as regards to property and other assets which they own, either together or separately. This may, for example, mean ordering the transfer and ownership of property from one civil partner to another for that persons benefit or the benefit of any children (known as property adjustment orders)
- The court can make an order in relation to the future pension entitlement of one of the civil partners in favour of the other. This order can relate to occupational pensions, personal pensions and other annuities (known as pension sharing orders)

Financial provision orders for maintenance can be made before a civil partnership has been ended or as a separation order granted by the court. Property adjustment and pension sharing orders only take legal effect once dissolution, separation or nullity order has been made by the court.

Even if the couple have been able to agree on maintenance and other property issues they should seek professional advice on such issues. In most cases the solicitor dealing with the end of the civil partnership will be able to provide appropriate advice.

If you require details of local solicitors with experience in this area you should go to www.communitylegaladvice.org.uk or phone the Community Legal Service on 0845 3454345.

Care of children

Part 2 Chapter 5 deals with the care of children. Agreeing arrangements for the care of any children should be the first priority of couples who are ending their civil partnerships or choosing to live apart through separation.

If a couple decide to end the civil partnership the court will want to ensure that both partners are happy with the arrangements for looking after children. If a couple are unable to agree the court will decide for them, or may do so, as part of the dissolution proceedings.

1

Introduction

Part 1 Civil Partnership

Subsection (1) Part 1 states that a civil partnership is a relationship between two people of the same sex ("civil partners")-

a) which is formed when they register as civil partners of each other-

    (i)   in England or Wales (under Part 2),

    (ii)   in Scotland (under Part 3),

    (iii)   in Northern Ireland (under Part 4), or

    (iv)   outside the United Kingdom under an Order in Council made under chapter 1 of Part 5 (registration at British Consulates etc, or by armed forces personnel), or

b) which they are treated under Chapter 2 of Part 5 as having formed (at the time determined under that Chapter) by virtue of having registered an overseas relationship.

Subsection (2) states that subsection (1) is subject to the provisions of this Act under or by virtue of which a civil partnership is void.

Subsection (3) states that a civil partnership ends only on death, dissolution or annulment.

Subsection (4) states that the references in subsection (3) to dissolution and annulment are to dissolution and annulment having effect under or recognised in accordance with this Act.

Subsection (5) states that references in this Act to an overseas relationship are to be read in accordance with Chapter 2 of Part 5.

2

Registration of Civil Partnerships

Part 2 Chapter 1 Civil Partnerships Act 2004.

Formation of civil partnerships by registration

Section 2 Part 2 of the Act deals with formation of civil partnerships by registration. Subsection (1) states that for the purposes of section 1, two people are to be regarded as having registered as civil partners of each other once each of them has signed the civil partnership document-

a) at the invitation of, and in the presence of, a civil partnership registrar, and
b) in the presence of each other and two witnesses.

Subsection (2) states that subsection 91) applies regardless of whether subsections (3) and (4) are complied with.

Subsection (3) states that after the civil partnership document has been signed under subsection (1), it must also be signed, in the presence of the civil partners and each other, by-

a) each of the two witnesses, and
b) the civil partnership registrar.

Subsection (4) states that after the witnesses and the civil partnership registrar have signed the civil partnership document, the relevant registration authority must ensure that-

a) the fact that the two people have registered as civil partners of each other, and

b) any other information prescribed by regulations,

is recorded in the register as soon as is practicable.

Subsection (5) states that no religious service is to be used while the civil partnership registrar is officiating at the signing of a civil partnership document.

Subsection (6) states that "the civil partnership document" has the meaning given by section 7(1).

Subsection (7) states that "the relevant registration authority" means the registration authority in whose area the registration takes place.

Eligibility

Section 3 deals with eligibility of partners to form a civil partnership. Subsection (1) states that two people are not eligible to register as civil partners of each other if

a) they are not of the same sex,
b) either of them is already a civil partner or lawfully married,
c) either of them is under 16, or
d) they are within prohibited degrees of relationship.

The definition of prohibited degrees of relationship is found in Schedule 1 to the Act and means essentially, closely related. There are absolute prohibitions and qualified prohibitions. See appendix for a list of Schedules to Act as outlined in this book. The schedules can be accessed through the government website mentioned in the overview to the Act.

Parental consent where proposed civil partner under 16

Section 4 deals with parental consent where the proposed civil partner is under 18. Although two people aged 16 or over can register for a civil partnership, subsection (1) of section 4 states that consent of an 'appropriate person' is required before a child under

16 and another person may register as civil partners The definition of appropriate person. is to be found in Schedule 2 of the Act.

The general registration procedure

Section 5 deals with the general registration procedure. There are a number of procedures under which two people may register as civil partners of each other: the standard procedure; the procedure for house bound persons; the procedure for detained persons and the special procedure which is designed for cases where people are seriously ill and not expected to recover.

Standard procedure

The standard procedure is used in most cases and where the other procedures do not apply.

Special procedure

Special procedures will apply where people are seriously ill, as described above. This will involve a variation to the standard procedure to encompass the circumstances of the illness.

The procedure for housebound persons

If one person is housebound there are special procedures to allow them to register a civil partnership at home. A statement has to be signed, by a doctor, confirming that this is the case and that the condition is likely to continue for the next three months. The statement must have been made no more than 14 days before notice being given and must be made on a standard form provided by the register office. The normal 15-day period (see below) will apply between giving notice and the civil partnership registration.

Detained persons

There are special procedures to allow a couple to register a civil partnership at a place where one of them is detained, for example a hospital or prison. The couple have to provide a statement, made by the prison governor or responsible person confirming that the place where a person is detained can be named in the notice of proposed civil partnership as the place where the registration is to take place. The statement must have been made no more than 21 days prior to notice being given. The normal 15 day waiting period applies (see below).

Place of registration

Section 6 of the Act outlines the place of registration for a civil partnership. Subsection (1) states that the place at which two people may register as civil partners of each other-

a) must be in England or Wales,
b) must not be in a religious premises, and
c) must be specified in the notices, or notice, of proposed civil partnership required by this chapter.

Subsection (2) states that "religious premises" means premises which-

a) are used solely or mainly for religious purposes, or
b) have been so used and have not been subsequently used solely or mainly for another purpose.

Subsection (3) states that in the case of registration under the standard procedure (including that procedure modified as mentioned in section 5), the place-

a) must be one which is open to any person wishing to attend the registration, and
b) before being specified in a notice of proposed civil partnership, must be agreed with the registration authority in the area where the place is located.

Subsection (4) states that if the place specified in a notice is not so agreed, the notice is void.

Subsection (5) states that a registration authority may provide a place in its area for the registration of civil partnerships.

The Civil partnership document

Section 7 deals with the civil partnership document. Subsection (1) of section 7 states that in this part "the civil partnership document" means-

a) in relation to the special procedure, a Registrar General's licence, and
b) in relation to any other procedure, a civil partnership schedule.

Subsection (2) states that before two people are entitled to register as civil partners of each other-

a) the civil partnership document must be delivered to the civil partnership registrar, and
b) the civil partnership registrar may then ask them for any information required (under section 2(4)) to be recorded in the register.

The standard procedure
Notice of proposed civil partnership and declaration

Section 8 of the Act deals with the notice of proposed civil partnership and declaration. Subsection (1) states that for two people to register as civil partners of each other under the standard procedure, each of them must:

a) give a notice of proposed civil partnership to a registration authority and
b) have resided in England or Wales for at least 7 days immediately before giving the notice.

Subsection (2) states that a notice of civil partnerships must contain prescribed information. This can be obtained from the appropriate register office.

Subsection (3) states that the notice must also include the necessary declaration, made and signed by the person giving the notice-

a) at the time when the notice is given, and
b) in the presence of an authorised person;

and the authorised person must attest the declaration by adding his/her name, description and place of residence.

Subsection (4) states that the necessary declaration is a solemn declaration in writing-

a) that the proposed civil partner believes that there is no impediment of kindred or affinity or other lawful hindrance to the formation of the civil partnership;
b) that each of the proposed civil partners has had a usual place of residence in England and Wales for at least 7 days before giving the notice.

Subsection (5) states that where a notice of civil partnership is given to a registration authority in accordance with this section, the registration authority must ensure that the following information is recorded in the register as soon as possible-

a) the fact that the notice has been given and the information in it;
b) the fact that the authorised person has attested the declaration.

Subsection (6) states that "authorised person" means an employee or officer or other person provided by a registration authority who is authorised by that authority to attest notices of proposed civil partnership.

Subsection (7) states that for the purposes of this Chapter, a notice of proposed civil partnership is recorded when subsection (5) is complied with.

Power to require evidence of name etc.
Section 9 deals with powers to require evidence of identity. Subsection (1) of section 9 states that the registration authority to

which a notice of proposed civil partnership is given may require the person giving the notice to provide it with specified evidence-

a) relating to that person, or
b) if the registration authority considers that the circumstances are exceptional, relating not only to that person but also to the persons proposed civil partner.

Subsection 92) states that such a requirement may be imposed at any time before the registration authority issues the civil partnership schedule under section 14.

Subsection (3) states that "specified evidence" in relation to a person, means such evidence as may be specified in guidance issued by the Registrar General-

a) of the persons name and surname
b) of the persons age,
c) as to whether the person has previously formed a civil partnership or marriage and, if so, as to the ending of the civil partnership or marriage,
d) of the persons nationality, and
e) as to the persons residence in England or Wales during the period of 7 days preceding the giving of a notice of proposed civil partnership by that person.

Proposed civil partnership to be publicised

Section 10 of the Act deals with the publication of the proposed partnership. Subsection (1) of section 10 states that where a notice of proposed civil partnership has been given to a registration authority, the relevant information must be publicised during the waiting period-

a) That registration authority
b) any registration authority in whose area the person giving the notice has resided during the period of 7 days preceding the giving of the notice,
c) by any registration authority in whose area the proposed

civil partner of the person giving the notice has resided during the period of 7 days preceding the giving of that notice

d) by the registration authority in whose area the place specified in the notice as the place of proposed registration is located and

e) by the Registrar General.

Subsection (2) states that "the relevant information" means-

a) the name of the person giving the notice,
b) the name of the person's proposed civil partner and
c) any other information prescribed by regulations.

Meaning of "the waiting period"

Section 11 deals with the meaning of the term waiting period. This mean the period-

a) beginning the day after the notice is recorded, and
b) subject to section 12, ending at the end of the period of 15 days beginning with that day.

Power to shorten the Waiting period

Section 12 deals with powers to shorten the waiting period. Subsection (1) of section 12 states that if the Registrar General, on an application being made to him, is satisfied that there are compelling reasons because of the exceptional circumstances of the case for shortening the period of 15 days mentioned in section 11 (b) he may shorten it to such period as he considers appropriate.

Subsection (2) states that regulations may make provision with respect to the making, and granting, of applications under subsection (1).

Subsection (3) states that regulations under subsection (2) may provide for-

a) the power conferred by subsection (1) to be exercised by a registration authority on behalf of the Registrar General in such classes of case as are prescribed by the regulations;

b) the making of an appeal to the Registrar General against a decision taken by a registration authority in accordance with regulations made by virtue of paragraph (a).

Objection to proposed civil partnership

Section 13 of Part 1 of the Act deals with likely objections to a proposed civil partnership. Subsection (1) states that any person may object to the issue of a proposed civil partnership by giving any registration authority notice of his objection. Subsection (2) states that a notice of objection must-

a) state the objector's place of residence and the grounds for objection, and

b) be signed on or on behalf of the objector.

Subsection (3) states that if a notice of objection is given to a registration authority, it must ensure that the fact that it has been given and the information in it are recorded in the register as soon as possible.

Issue of civil partnership schedule

Section 14 of the Act deals with the issue of a 'schedule' or permission to marry. This is issued after the waiting period and after the registration authority is satisfied that there are no objections to the civil partnership. If the registration authority is not satisfied that the proposed partnership should go ahead then it will not issue a schedule. This could be on the grounds of information provided or on the grounds of an objection, which must be investigated.

Appeal against refusal to issue civil partnership schedule

Section 15 deals with the proposed civil partners right to appeal against refusal to issue a schedule.

Frivolous objections and representations

Section 16 deals with the powers of the registration authority in the event of frivolous objections and representations.

Period during which registration may take place

Section 17 deals with the period during which registration can take place. Subsection (1) states that the proposed civil partners may not register as civil partners of each other on the production of the civil partnership schedule until the waiting period in relation to each notice of proposed civil partnership has expired. Subsection (2) states that subject to subsection (1) under the standard procedure, they may register as civil partners by signing the civil partnership schedule at any time during the applicable period.

Subsection (3) states that if they do not register as civil partners by signing the civil partnership schedule before the end of the applicable period-

a) the notices of proposed civil partnership and the civil partnership schedule are void, and
b) no civil partnership registrar may officiate at the signing of the civil partnership schedule by them.

Subsection (4) states that the applicable period, in relation to two people registering as civil partners of each other, is the period of 12 months beginning with-

a) the day on which notices of proposed civil partnership are recorded, or
b) if the notices are not recorded on the same day, the earlier of those days.

Housebound persons

Section 18 deals with housebound persons. Subsection (1) of section 18 states that this section applies if two people wish to register as civil partners of each other at the place where one of them is housebound.

Subsection (2) states that a person is housebound at any place if, in relation to that person, a statement is made by a registered medical practitioner that, in his opinion-

a) because of illness or disability, that person ought not to move or be moved from the place where he is at the time when the statement is made, and
b) it is likely to be the case for the next three months that because of the illness or disability that person ought not to move or be moved from that place.

Subsection (3) states that the procedure under which the two people concerned may register as civil partners of each other is the same as the standard procedure except that-

a) each notice of proposed civil partnership must be accompanied by a statement under subsection (2) ("a medical statement"), which must have been made not more than 14 days before the day on which the notice is recorded,
b) the fact that the registration authority to whom the notice is given has received the medical statement must be recorded in the register, and
c) the applicable period (for the purposes of section 17) is the period of 3 months beginning with-

(i) the day on which the notices of proposed civil partnership are recorded, or
(ii) if the notices are not recorded on the same day, the earlier of those days.

Subsection (4) states that a medical statement must contain such information and must be made in such a manner as may be prescribed by regulations.

Subsection (5) states that a medical statement may not be made in relation to a person who is detained as described in section 19 (2).

Subsection (6) states that for the purposes of this chapter, a person in relation to whom a medical statement is made is to be treated, if he would not otherwise be treated, as resident and usually resident at the place where he is for the time being.

Detained persons

Section 19 deals with detained persons. Subsection (1) states that this section applies if two people wish to register as civil partners of each other at the place where one of them is detained.

Subsection (2) defines "detained" as-

a) as patient in a hospital (but otherwise than by virtue of section 2, 4, 5, 35 or 136 of the Mental Health Act 1983 (c.20) (short term detentions), or
b) in a prison or other place to which the Prison Act 1952 (c.52) applies.

Subsection (3) states that the procedure under which the two people concerned may register as civil partners of each other is the same as the standard procedure, except that-

a) each notice of proposed civil partnership must be accompanied by a supporting statement, which must have been made not more than 21 days before the day on which the notice is recorded,
b) the fact that the registration authority that the notice is given has received the supporting statement must be recorded in the register ,and
c) the applicable period (for the purposes of section 17) is the period of 3 months beginning with-

   (i)   the day on which the notices of proposed civil partnership are recorded, or
   (ii)   if the notices are not recorded on the same day, the earlier of those days.

Subsection (4) states that a supporting statement, in relation to a detained person, is a statement made by the responsible authority which-

a) identifies the establishment where the person is detained, and
b) states that the responsible authority has no objection to that establishment being specified in a notice of proposed civil partnership as the place at which the person is to register as a civil partner.

Subsection (5) states that a supporting statement must contain such information and must be made in such a manner as may be prescribed by regulations.

Subsection (6) defines "the responsible authority as-

a) if the person is detained in a hospital, the hospital's managers,
b) if the person is detained in a prison or other place to which the 1952 Act applies, the governor or other officer for the time being in charge of that prison or other place.

Subsection (7) defines "patient" and "hospital" as having the same meaning as in Part 2 of the 1983 Act and "managers" in relation to a hospital, has the same meaning as in section 145(1) of the 1983 Act.

Subsection (8) states that for the purposes of this Chapter, a detained person is to be treated, if he would not be otherwise so treated, as resident and usually resident at the place where he is for the time being.

Modified procedures for certain non- residents

Section 20 deals with modified procedures for certain non-residents. Subsection (1) states that subsection (5) applies in the following 3 cases.

Subsection (2) is where two people wish to register as civil partners of each other in England and Wales and one of them (A) resides in Scotland and the other in England or Wales (B)

Subsection (3) is where two people wish to register as civil partners of each other in England and Wales and one of them (A) resides in Northern Ireland and the other (B) resides in England or Wales;

Subsection (4) is where two people wish to register as civil partners of each other in England and Wales and one of them (A) is a member of Her Majesty's armed forces who is serving outside the United Kingdom and the other (B) resides in England and Wales.

Subsection (5) states that for the purposes of the standard procedure, the procedure for house-bound persons and the procedure for detained persons-

a) A is not required to give a notice of proposed civil partnership under this chapter;

b) B may give a notice of proposed civil partnership and make the necessary declaration without regard to the requirement that would otherwise apply that A must reside in England or Wales;

c) The waiting period is calculated by reference to the day on which B's notice is recorded;

d) The civil partnership schedule is not to be issued by a registration authority unless A or B produces to that registration authority a certificate of no impediment issued to A under the relevant provision;

e) The applicable period is calculated by reference to the day on which B's notice is recorded and, where the standard procedure is used in the first and second cases, is the period of 3 months beginning with that day;

f) Section 31 applies as if in subsections (1)(a) and (2)(c) for "each notice" there were substituted "B's notice".

Subsection (6) states that the "relevant provision" means-

a) if A resides in Scotland, section 97;
b) if A resides in Northern Ireland, section 150;
c) if A is a member of Her Majesty's armed forces who is serving outside the United Kingdom, section 239.

Subsection (7) states that "Her Majesty's forces" has the same meaning as in the Army Act 1955 (3 and 4 Eliz. 2 c.18).

The special procedure

Notice of proposed civil partnership

Section 21 of the Act deals with the special procedure and notices of proposed civil partnership. Subsection (1) of section 21 states that for two people to register as civil partners of each other under the special procedure, one of them must-

a) give a notice of proposed civil partnership to the registration authority for the area in which it is proposed that the registration takes place, and
b) comply with any requirement made under section 22.

Subsection (2) states that the notice must contain such information as may be prescribed by regulations.

Subsection (3) states that subsections (3) to (6) of section 8 (necessary declarations etc.) apart from paragraph (b) of subsection (4), apply for the purposes of this section as they apply for purposes of that section.

Evidence to be produced

Section 22 deals with evidence to be produced under the special procedure. Subsection (1) of section 22 states that the person giving a notice of proposed civil procedure must produce to the authority such evidence as the Registrar General may require to satisfy him-

a) that there is no lawful impediment to the formation of the civil partnership,
b) that the conditions in subsection (2) are met, and
c) that there is sufficient reason why a licence should be granted.

Subsection (2) states that the conditions are that one of the proposed civil partners-

a) is seriously ill and not expected to recover, and
b) understands the nature and purport of signing a Registrar General's licence.

Subsection (3) states that the certificate of a registered medical practitioner is sufficient evidence of any or all of the matters referred to in subsection (2).

Application to be reported to Registrar General

Section 24 deals with applications which must be reported to the Registrar General. On receiving notice of proposed civil partnership under section 21 and any evidence under section 22, the registration authority must-

a) inform the Registrar General, and
b) comply with any directions the Registrar General may give for verifying the evidence given.

Objection to issue of Registrar General's notice

Section 24 deals with objections. Subsection (1) of section 24 states that any person may object to the Registrar General giving authority for the issue of his licence by giving the Registrar General or any registration authority notice of his objection.

Subsection (2) states that a notice of objection must-

a) state the objector's place of residence and the ground of objection, and
b) be signed on or on behalf of the objector.

Subsection (3) states that if a notice of objection is given to a registration authority, it must ensure that the fact that it has been given and the information in it are recorded in the register as soon as possible.

Issue of Registrar General's notice

Section 25 deals with the issue of notice. Subsection (1) of section 25 states that this section applies where a notice of proposed civil partnership is given to a registration authority under section 21.

Subsection (2) states that the registration authority may issue a Registrar General's licence if, and only if, given authority to do so by the Registrar General.

Subsection (3) states that the Registrar General-

a) may not give his authority unless he is satisfied that one of the proposed civil partners is seriously ill and not expected to recover, but

b) if so satisfied, must give his authority unless a lawful impediment to the issue of his licence has been shown to his satisfaction to exist.

Subsection (4) states that a licence under this section must state that it is issued on the authority of the Registrar General.

Subsection (5) states that regulations may (subject to subsection (4)) make provision as to the contents of a licence under this section.

Subsection (6) states that if an objection has been made to the Registrar General giving authority for the issue of his licence, he is not to give that authority until-

a) he has investigated the objection and decided whether it ought to obstruct the issue of his licence, or

b) the objection has been withdrawn by the person who made it.

Subsection (7) states that any decision of the Registrar General under subsection (6)(a) is final.

Frivolous objections: liability for costs

Section 26 deals with frivolous objections. Subsection (1) states that this section applies if-

a) a person objects to the Registrar General giving authority for the issue of his licence, but
b) the Registrar General declares that the grounds on which the objection is made arc frivolous and ought not to obstruct the issue of his licence.

Subsection (2) states that the person who made the objection is liable for-

a) any costs of the proceedings before the Registrar General, and
b) damages recoverable by the proposed civil partner to whom the objection relates.

Subsection (3) states that for the purpose of enabling any person to recover any such costs and damages, a copy of a declaration of the Registrar General purporting to be sealed with the seal of the General Register Office is evidence that the Registrar General has made the declaration.

Period during which registration may take place

Section 27 deals with the period during which registration may take place. Subsection (1) of section 27 states that if a Registrar General's licence has been issued under section 25, the proposed civil partners may register as civil partners by signing it at any time within 1 month from the day on which the notice of proposed civil partnership was given.

Subsection (2) states that if they do not register as civil partners by signing the licence within the 1 month period-

a) the notice of proposed civil partnership and the licence are void, and
b) no civil partnership registrar may officiate at the signing of the licence by them.

Supplementary

Registration authorities

Section 28 deals with definitions of registration authority. In this chapter "registration authority" means-

a) in relation to England, a county council, the council of any district comprised in an area for which there is no county council, a London borough council, the Common Council of the City of London or the Council of the Isles of Scilly;
b) in relation to Wales, a county council or a county borough council.

Civil partnership registrars

Section 29 deals with civil partnership registrars. Subsection (1) states that a civil partnership registrar is an individual who is designated by a registration authority as a civil partnership registrar for its area.

Subsection (2) states that it is the duty of each registration authority to ensure that there is a sufficient number of civil partnership registrars for its area to carry out in that area the functions of civil partnership registrars.

Subsection (3) states that each registration authority must inform the registrar general as soon as is practicable-

a) of any designation it has made of a person as a civil partnership registrar, and
b) the ending of any such designation.

Subsection (4) states that the Registrar General must make available to the public a list-

a) of civil partnership registrars, and
b) of the registration authorities for which they are designated to act.

The Registrar General and the register

Section 30 deals with the Registrar General. Subsection (1) of section 30 states that in this chapter the "Registrar General" means the Registrar General for England and Wales.

Subsection (2) states that the Registrar General must provide a system for keeping any records that relate to civil partnerships and are required by this Chapter to be made.

Subsection (3) states that the system may, in particular, enable those records to be kept together with other records kept by the Registrar General.

Subsection (4) states that in this Chapter "the register" means the system for keeping records provided under subsection (2).

Offences relating to civil partnership schedule

Section 31 relates to offences and the civil partnership schedule. Subsection (1) states that a person commits an offence if he issues a civil partnership schedule knowing that he does so-

a) before the waiting period in relation to each notice of proposed civil partnership has expired,
b) after the end of the applicable period, and
c) at a time when its issue has been forbidden under Schedule 2 by a person entitled to forbid its issue.

Subsection (2) states that a person commits an offence if, in his actual or purported capacity as a civil partnership registrar, he officiates at the signing of a civil partnership schedule by proposed civil partners knowing that he does so-

a) at a place other than the place specified in the notices of proposed civil partnership and the civil partnership schedule,

b) in the absence of a civil partnership registrar,

c) before the waiting period in relation to each notice of proposed civil partnership has expired, or

d) even though the civil partnership is void under section 49 (b) or (c).

Subsection (3) states that a person guilty of an offence under subsection (1) or (2) is liable on conviction on indictment to imprisonment for a term not exceeding 5 years or to a fine (or both).

Subsection (4) states that a prosecution under this section may not be commenced more than 3 years after the commission of the offence.

Offences relating to Registrar General's notice

Section 32 deals with offences relating to the Registrar General's licences. Subsection (1) states that a person commits an offence if-

a) he gives information by way of evidence in response to a requirement under s 22(1), knowing that the information is false;

b) he gives a certificate as provided for by section 22(3) knowing that the certificate is false;

Subsection (2) states that a person commits an offence if, in his actual or purported capacity as a civil partnership registrar, he officiates at the signing of a Registrar General's licence by proposed civil partners knowing that he does so-

a) at a place other than the place specified in the licence,

b) in the absence of a civil partnership registrar,

c) after the end of 1 month from the day on which the notice of proposed civil partnership was given, or

41

d) even though the civil partnership is void under section 49 (b) or (c).

Subsection (3) states that a person guilty of an offence under subsection (1) or (2) is liable-

a) on conviction on indictment, to imprisonment not exceeding 3 years or to a fine or both,
b) on summary conviction, to a fine not exceeding the statutory maximum.

Subsection (4) states that a prosecution under this section may not be commenced more than 3 years after the commission of the offence.

Offences relating to the recording of a civil partnership

Section 33 deals with offences relating to the recording of a civil partnership. Subsection (1) states that a civil partnership registrar commits an offence if he refuses or fails to comply with the provisions of this Chapter or of any regulations made under section 36.

Subsection (2) states that a civil partnership registrar guilty of an offence under subsection (1) is liable-

a) on conviction on indictment, to imprisonment for a term not exceeding 2 years or to a fine or both;
b) on summary conviction, to a fine not exceeding the statutory maximum;

and on conviction shall cease to be a civil partnership registrar.

Subsection (3) states that a person commits an offence if-

a) under arrangements made by a registration authority for the purposes of section 2 (4) , he is under a duty to record information required to be recorded under section 2 (4), but
b) he refuses or without reasonable cause omits to do so.

Subsection (4) states that a person guilty of an offence under subsection (3) is liable on summary conviction to a fine not exceeding level 3 on the standard scale.

Subsection (5) states that a person commits an offence if he records in the register information relating to the formation of a civil partnership by the signing of a civil partnership schedule, knowing that the civil partnership is void under section 49 (b) or (c).

Subsection (6) states that a person guilty of an offence under subsection (5) is liable on conviction or indictment, to imprisonment for a term not exceeding 5 years or to a fine or both.

Subsection (7) states that a person commits an offence if he records in the register information relating to the formation of a civil partnership by the signing of a Registrar General's licence, knowing that the civil partnership is void under section 49(b) or (c).

Subsection (8) states that a person guilty of an offence under subsection (7) is liable-

a) on conviction on indictment, to imprisonment for a term not exceeding three years or to a fine or both;
b) on summary conviction, to a fine not exceeding the statutory maximum.

Subsection (9) states that a prosecution under subsection (5) or (7) may not be commenced more than 3 years after the commission of the offence.

Fees

Section 34 deals with fees. See introduction for a breakdown of fees payable. Section 34 outlines the powers of the Chancellor of the Exchequer to set fees and the powers of the Registrar General to remit fees in cases of hardship. Section 35 and 36 deal with powers to assimilate provisions relating to civil registration (35) and regulations and orders (36).

3

Dissolution of Civil Partnerships

Part 2. Chapter 2

Dissolution of a Civil Partnership, Nullity and Other Proceedings.

Section 37 of chapter 2 of the Civil Partnerships Act 2004 deals with the ending of a civil partnership, either through dissolution or nullity or other.

As with marriage, problems may arise and partners to a civil partnership may wish to terminate the union. Likewise, the union may not, for some reason, be legal and may be annulled. Later chapters deal with economic and other matters which will arise after dissolution.

By virtue of Chapter 2, the court may:

a) make a dissolution order which dissolves a civil partnership on the ground that it has broken down irretrievably;
b) make a nullity order which annuls a civil partnership which is void or voidable;
c) make a presumption of death order which dissolves a civil partnership on the ground that one of the civil partners is presumed to be dead;
d) make a separation order which provides for the separation of the civil partners.

Further, every dissolution, nullity or presumption of death order:

a) is, in the first instance, a conditional order and;

b) may not be made final before the end of the prescribed period (see below).

A nullity order made where a civil partnership is voidable annuls the civil partnership only as respects any time after the order, and the civil partnership is to be treated (despite the order) as if it had existed up to that time.

Courts can be the High Court or, if the County Court has jurisdiction by virtue of Part 5 of the Matrimonial and Family Proceedings Act 1984, a county court.

The period before conditional orders can be made final

Section 38 of the Act states that the prescribed period referred to above is:

a) 6 weeks from the making of the conditional order, or
b) if the 6-week period would end on a day on which the office or the registry dealing with the case is closed, the period of 6 weeks extended to the first day on which the offices are next open.

This prescribed period can be replaced with a different definition by the Lord Chancellor. Six months, however, will be the maximum prescribed period. In a particular case, the court dealing with the case can shorten the prescribed period. Any instrument carrying such an order is subject to annulment by a resolution of either houses of parliament.

Intervention of the Queen's proctor

This section, 39, will apply if an application has been made for a dissolution, nullity or presumption of death order. The court may, if it thinks fit, direct all necessary papers are to be sent to the Queen's proctor who must under the directions of the Attorney General instruct counsel to argue before the court any question in relation to the matter which the court considers it necessary or expedient to have fully argued.

If any person at any time either during the progress of the proceedings or before the conditional order is made final gives information to the Queen's Proctor on any matter material to the due decision of the case, the Queen's proctor may take such steps as the Attorney general considers necessary or expedient.

If the Queen's Proctor does intervene the courts can award costs of such an intervention against appropriate parties.

Proceedings before an order has been made final

Section 40 deals with any proceedings or events prior to an order being made final. The section applies if a conditional order has been made and the Queen's proctor or any other person who has not been party to a proceedings in which an order was made, shows cause why the order should not be made final on the ground that material facts have not been brought before the court. The section also applies if:

a) a conditional order has been made,
b) three months have elapsed since the earliest date on which an application could have been made for the order to be made final,
c) no such application has been made by the civil partner who applied for the conditional order, and
d) the other civil partner makes an application to the court under this section.

The court may:

a) make the order final
b) rescind the order
c) require further enquiry
d) other wise deal with the case as it thinks fit.

Time bar on application for dissolution orders

Section 41 of the Act deals with time limits on applications for orders. No application for a dissolution order may be made to the court before the end of the period of one year from the formation of the civil partnership. Nothing in the section prevents an application being made which includes matters that happened before the end of the 1-year period.

Attempts at reconciliation of civil partners

Section 42 of the Act applies where an application has been made for a dissolution or separation order. The rules of the court must make provision for requiring the solicitor acting for the applicant to certify whether he or she has discussed with the applicant the possibility of a reconciliation with the civil partner and given the applicant the name and address of persons qualified to act in helping to effect a reconciliation of the civil partners. If at any stage of the proceedings it seems to the court that there is a reasonable possibility of a reconciliation between the civil partners, the court may adjourn the proceedings for such period as it thinks fit to enable attempts to be made to effect a reconciliation between them.

Consideration by the court of any agreements or arrangements

Section 43 applies in cases where proceedings for a dissolution or separation order is contemplated or have begun and an agreement or arrangement is made or proposed to be made between the civil partners which relates to, arises out of, or is connected with, the proceedings. The civil partners, or either of them, can refer the arrangement to court and the court will consider the arrangement.

Dissolution of a civil partnership which has broken down irretrievably

Subject to section 41, under section 44 of the Act, an application for a dissolution order may be made to the court by either civil partner on the ground that the civil partnership has broken down irretrievably. On an application for a dissolution order the court must inquire, as far as it reasonably can, into:

a)   the facts alleged by the applicant, and
b)   the facts alleged by the respondent.

The court hearing an application for a dissolution order must not hold that the civil partnership has broken down irretrievably unless the applicant satisfies the court of one or more of the facts described below (sub section 5(a), (b), (c) or (d)). If the court is satisfied of any of the facts described below it must make a dissolution order unless it is satisfied on all the evidence that the partnership has not broken down irretrievably.

The facts laid out in subsection 5(a) (b) (c) or (d) of section 41 of the act are:

a) that the respondent has behaved in such a way that the applicant cannot reasonably be expected to live with the respondent;

b) that:

    (i)   the applicant and the respondent have lived apart for a continuous period of at least 2 years immediately preceding the making of the application (2 years separation), and

    (ii) the respondent consents to a dissolution order being made;

c) that the applicant and the respondent have lived apart for a continuous period of at least 5 years immediately preceding the making of the application (5 years separation);

d) that the respondent has deserted the applicant for a continuous period of at least 2 years immediately preceding the making of the application.

Supplemental provisions as to facts raising presumption of breakdown

Section 45 of the Act relates to additional facts that effect the making of an order for a dissolution of a civil partnership.

a) in any proceedings for a dissolution order the applicant alleges, in reliance on s44 (5)(a) that the respondent has behaved in such a way that the applicant cannot reasonably be expected to live with the respondent, but

b) after the date of the occurrence of the final incident relied on by the applicant and held by the court to support his allegation, the applicant and the respondent have lived together for a period (or period) which does not, or which taken together do not, exceed 6 months.

The fact that the applicant and respondent have lived together as mentioned in subsection (b) must be disregarded in determining, for the purposes of 44(5)(b) whether the applicant cannot reasonably be expected to live with the respondent.

Section 45 states that the rules of the court must make provision for the purpose of ensuring that the respondent has been given such information as will enable him or her to understand the consequences to him of consenting to the making of the order and the steps which he or she must take to indicate consent.

For the purposes of section 44(5)(d) the court may treat a period of desertion as having continued at a time when the deserting partner was incapable of continuing the necessary intention, if the evidence before the court is such that, had he not been so incapable, the court would have inferred that the desertion would have continued at that time.

In considering for the purposes of section 44(5) whether the period for which the civil partners have lived apart or the period for which the respondent has deserted the applicant has been continuous, no account is to be taken of :

a) any one period not exceeding 6 months, or
b) any two or more periods no exceeding 6 months in all, during which the civil partners resumed living with each other.

But no period during which the civil partners have lived with each other counts as part of the period during which the civil partners have lived apart as part of the period of desertion.

Dissolution order not precluded by previous separation order etc

Section 46 of the Act states that subsections (1) (2) and (3) apply if any of the following orders has been made in relation to a civil partnership:

a) a separation order;

b) an order under schedule 6 to the Act (financial relief in magistrates courts etc)

c) an order under section 33 of the Family Law Act 1966 (c.27) (occupation orders)

d) an order under section 37 of the 1996 Act (orders where neither civil partner entitled to share the home)

Subsection (2) states that nothing prevents either civil partner from applying for a dissolution order or the court from making a dissolution order on the same facts, or substantially the same facts, as those proved in support of the making of the order referred to above.

Subsection (3) section 46 states that on the application for the dissolution order the court may treat the order referred to above as sufficient proof of any desertion or other fact by reference to which it was made but must not make the dissolution order without receiving evidence from the applicant.

Subsection (4) states that if the application for the dissolution order follows a separation order or any order requiring the civil partners to live apart, and there was a degree of desertion immediately preceding the institution of the proceedings for the separation order, and the civil partners have not resumed living together and the separation order has continuously been in force since it was made, then the period of desertion is to be treated for the purposes of the application of the dissolution order as if it had immediately preceded the making of the application.

Subsection (5) states that for the purposes of s (44)(5)(d) the court may treat as a period during which the respondent has deserted the applicant any period during which there was in force:

a) an injunction granted by the high court or a county court which excludes the respondent from the civil partnership home, or

b) an order under section 33 or 37 of the 1996 Act which prohibits the respondent from occupying a dwelling house in which the applicant and the respondent have or at any time have had, a civil partnership home.

Refusal of dissolution in 5-year separation cases on grounds of grave hardship

Section 47 deals with the opposing of a dissolution order by the respondent. Subsection (1) states that the respondent to an application for a dissolution order in which the applicant alleges 5 years separation may oppose the making of the order on the grounds that:

a) the dissolution of the civil partnership will result in grave or other financial hardship to him/her, and,

b) it would in all the circumstances be wrong to dissolve the civil partnership.

Subsection (2) states that subsection (3) (below) applies if:

a) the making of a dissolution order is opposed under this section,

b) the court finds that the applicant is entitled to rely in support of his application on the fact of 5 years separation and makes no such finding as to any other fact mentioned in section 44(5), and

c) apart from this section, the court would make a dissolution order.

Subsection 3 states that the court must consider all the circumstances, including the conduct of the civil partners and the interests of the civil partners and any of the children or other persons concerned, and if it is of the opinion that the ground mentioned in subsection 1 is made out, dismiss the application for the dissolution order.

Subsection (4) further defines 'hardship' as including the loss of the chance of acquiring any benefit which the respondent might acquire if the civil partnership were not dissolved.

Proceedings before order made final: protection for respondent in separation cases

Section 48 of the Act deals with the protection of the respondent in separation cases. Subsection (1) states that the court may, on application made by the respondent, rescind a conditional dissolution order if:

a) it made the order on the basis of a finding that the applicant was entitled to rely on the fact of 2 years separation coupled with the respondents consent to a dissolution order being made,

b) it made no such finding as to any other fact mentioned in section 44(5) and

c) it is satisfied that the applicant misled the respondent (whether intentionally or unintentionally) about any matter which the respondent took into account when deciding to give his consent.

Subsection 2 of section 48 states that subsections (3) to (5) apply if:

a) the respondent to an application for a dissolution order in which the applicant alleged:

    (i)   2 years separation coupled with the respondent's consent to a dissolution order being made, or

    (ii)   5 years separation

has applied to the court for consideration under subsection (3) of his financial position after the dissolution of the civil partnership, and

b) the court:

   (i) has made a conditional dissolution order on the basis of a finding that the applicant was entitled to rely in support of his application on the fact of 2 years or 5 years separation, and

   (ii) has made no such finding as to any other fact mentioned in section 44(5).

Subsection (3) of section 48 states that the court hearing an application by the respondent under subsection (2) must consider all the circumstances, including:

a) the health, age, conduct, earning capacity, financial resources and financial obligations of each of the parties, and

b) the financial position of the respondent as, having regard to the dissolution it is likely to be after the death of the applicant should the applicant die first.

Subsection (4) states that, subject to subsection (5) the court must not make an order final unless it is satisfied that:

a) the applicant should not be required to make any financial provision for the respondent, or

b) the financial provision made by the applicant for the respondent is-

   (i) fair and reasonable

   (ii) the best that can be made in the circumstances.

Subsection (5) states that the court may if it thinks fit make the order final if:

a) it appears that there are circumstances making it desirable that the order should be made final without delay, and

b) it has obtained a satisfactory undertaking from the applicant that he will make such financial provision for the respondent as it may approve.

Nullity

Grounds on which a civil partnership is void

Section 49 deals with nullity of a civil partnership. Nullity effectively means a void civil partnership.

Where two people register as civil partners of each other in England and Wales, the civil partnership is void if:

a) at the time when they do so, they are not eligible to register as civil partners under Chapter 1,

b) at the time when they do so they both know-

    (i)   that the notice of proposed civil partnership has not been given,

    (ii)   that the civil partnership document has not been duly issued,

    (iii)   that the civil partnership document is void

    (iv)   that the place of registration is a place other than that specified in the notices (or notice) of proposed civil partnership and the civil partnership document, or

    (v)   that a civil partnership registrar is not present, or

c) the civil partnership document is void under paragraph 6 (5) of Schedule 2 to the Act (civil partnership between child and another person forbidden). .

Grounds on which civil partnership is voidable

Section 50 of the Act deals with grounds on which a civil partnership can be voided. Subsection (1) states that where two people register as civil partners of each other in England and Wales, the civil partnership is voidable if:

a) either of them did not validly consent to its formation (whether as a result of duress, mistake, unsoundness of mind or otherwise)

b) at the time of its formation either of them, though capable of giving a valid consent, was suffering, whether continuously or intermittently, from mental disorder of such a kind or to such an extent as to be unfitted for civil partnership;

c) at the time of its formation, the respondent was pregnant by some person other than the applicant;

d) an interim gender recognition certificate under the Gender Recognition Act 2004 (c.7) has, after the time of its formation, been issued to either civil partner;

e) the respondent is a person whose gender at the time of its formation had become the acquired gender under the 2004 Act.

(2) In this section and section 51 'mental disorder' has the same meaning as in the Mental Health Act 1983 (c.20).

Bars to relief where civil partnership is voidable

Section 51 deals with relief in relation to making a nullity order. Subsection (1) of section 51 states that the court must not make a nullity order on the ground that a civil partnership is voidable if the respondent satisfies the court:

a) that the applicant, with knowledge that it was open to him to obtain a nullity order, conducted himself in relation to the respondent in such a way as to lead the respondent reasonably to believe that he would not seek to do so, and

b) that it would be unjust to the respondent to make the order.

Subsection 2 states that, without prejudice to subsection (1) the court must not make a nullity order by virtue of section 50(1)(a),(b)(C) or(e) unless-

a) it is satisfied that proceedings were instituted within 3 years from the date of the formation of the civil partnership, or

b) leave for the institution of proceedings after the end of that 3 year period has been granted under subsection (3).

Subsection (3) states that a judge of the court may, on an application made to him, grant leave for the intention of proceedings if he:

a) is satisfied that the applicant has at some time during the three year period suffered from mental disorder, and

b) considers that in all the circumstances of the case it would be just to grant leave for the institution of the proceedings.

Subsection (4) states that an application for leave under subsection (3) may be made after the end of the 3 year period.

Subsection (5) states that, without prejudice to subsection (1) the court must not make a nullity order by virtue of section 50(1)(d) unless it is satisfied that proceedings were instituted within the period of 6 months from the date of issue of the interim gender recognition certificate.

Subsection (6) states that, without prejudice to subsection (1) and (2) the court must not make a nullity order by virtue of section 50(1)(c) or (e) unless it is satisfied that the applicant was at the time of the formation of the civil partnership ignorant of the facts alleged.

Proof of certain matters not necessary to validity of civil partnership

Section 52, subsection (1) of the Act states that where two people have registered as civil partners of each other in England and Wales, it is not necessary in support of the civil partnership to give any proof:

a) that any person whose consent to the civil partnership was required under section 4 (parental etc. consent) had given his consent, or

b) that the civil partnership registrar was designated as such by the registration authority in whose area the registration took place;

and no evidence is to be given to prove the contrary in any proceedings touching the validity of the civil partnership.

Power to validate civil partnership

Section 53 of the Act deals with powers to validate a civil partnership. Subsection (1) of section 53 states that where two people have registered as civil partners of each other in England and Wales, the Lord Chancellor may by order validate the civil partnership if it appears to him that it is or may be void under section 49(b).

Subsection (2) states that an order under subsection (1) may include provisions for relieving a person from any liability under section 31(2) 32(2) 0r 33(5) or (7).

Subsection (3) states that the draft of an order under subsection (1) must be advertised, in such manner as the Lord Chancellor thinks fit, not less than one month before the order is made.

Subsection (4) states that the Lord Chancellor must:

a) consider all objections to the order sent to him in writing during that month, and
b) if it appears to him necessary, direct a local enquiry into the validity of any such objections.

Subsection (5) states that an order under subsection (1) is subject to special parliamentary procedure.

Validity of civil partnerships registered outside England and Wales

Section 54 of the Act deals with civil partnerships registered outside England and Wales. Subsection (1) of section 54 states that where two people register as civil partners of each other in Scotland, the civil partnership is-

a) void, if it would be void in Scotland under section 123, and
b) voidable, if the circumstances fall within section 50(1)(d).

Subsection (2) states that where two people register as civil partners of each other in Northern Ireland, the civil partnership is-

57

a) void, if it would be void in Northern Ireland under section 173, and

b) voidable, if circumstances fall within any paragraph of section 50(1).

Subsection (3) states that subsection (4) below applies where two people register as civil partners of each other under an order in Council under-

a) section 210 (registration at British consulates etc,) or

b) section 211 (registration by armed forces personnel),

(the 'relevant section')

Subsection (4) states that the civil partnership is-

a) void, if-

(i) the condition in subsection (2) (a) 0r (b) of the relevant section is not met, or

(ii) a requirement prescribed for the purposes of this paragraph by an Order in Council under the relevant section is not complied with, and

(b) voidable if,

(i) the appropriate part of the United Kingdom is England and Wales or Northern Ireland and the circumstances fall within any paragraph of section 50(1), or

(ii) the appropriate part of the United Kingdom is Scotland and the circumstances fall within section 50(1)(d).

Subsection (5) states that the appropriate part of the United kingdom is the part by reference to which the condition in subsection (2)(b) of the relevant section is met.

Subsection (6) states that subsections (7) and (8) below apply where two people have registered an apparent or alleged overseas relationship.

(7) The civil partnership is void if-

a) the relationship is not an overseas relationship, or
b) (even though the relationship is an overseas relationship) the parties are not treated under chapter 2 of part 5 as having formed a civil partnership.

(8) The civil partnership is voidable if-

a) the overseas relationship is voidable under section 50(1)(d), or
b) the circumstances fall within section 50(1)(d), or
c) where either of the parties was domiciled in England and Wales or Northern Ireland at the time when the overseas relationship was registered, the circumstances fall within section 50(1)(a)(b)(c)or(e)

Presumption of death orders

Section 55 of the Act deals with presumption of death orders. Subsection (1) states that the court may, on an application made by a civil partner, make a presumption of death order if it is satisfied that reasonable grounds exist for supposing that the other civil partner is dead.

Subsection (2) states that, in any proceedings under this section the fact that:

a) for a period of 7 years or more the civil partner has been continually absent from the applicant, and
b) the applicant has no reason to believe that the other civil partner has been living within that time.

is evidence that the other civil partner is dead until the contrary is proved.

Separation orders

Section 56 deals with separation orders. Subsection (1) of section 56 states that an application for a separation order may be made to the court by either civil partner on the ground that any such fact as is mentioned in section 44(5)(a),(b),(c) or (d) exists.

Subsection (2) states that on an application for a separation order the court must inquire, so far as it reasonably can, into-

a) the facts alleged by the applicant, and
b) any facts alleged by the respondent,

but whether the civil partnership has broken down irretrievably is irrelevant.

Subsection (3) states that, if the court is satisfied on the evidence of any such fact as mentioned in section 44(5)(a),(b),(c) or (d) it must, subject to section 63, make a separation order.

Subsection (4) states that section 45 (supplemental provisions as to facts raising presumption of breakdown) applies for the purposes of an application for a separation order alleging any such fact as it applies in relation to an application for a dissolution order alleging that fact.

Effect of a separation order

Section 57 deals with the effect of a separation order. If either civil partner dies intestate as respects all or any of his or her real or personal property while a separation order is in force and the separation is continuing, the property as respects which he or she died intestate devolves as if the other civil partner had then been dead.

Declarations

Section 58 of the Act deals with declarations. Subsection (1) of section 58 states that any person may apply to the high court or a county court for one or more of the following declarations in relation to a civil partnership specified in the application:

a) a declaration that the civil partnership was at its inception a valid civil partnership;
b) a declaration that the civil partnership subsisted on a date specified in the application;
c) a declaration that the civil partnership did not subsist on a date so specified;
d) a declaration that the validity of a dissolution, annulment or legal separation obtained outside England and Wales in respect of the civil partnership is entitled to recognition in England and Wales;
e) a declaration that the validity of a dissolution, annulment or legal separation so obtained in respect of the civil partnership is not entitled to recognition in England and Wales.

Subsection (2) of section 58 states that where an application under subsection (1) is made to a court by a person other than a civil partner in the civil partnership to which the application relates, the court must refuse to hear the application if it considers that the applicant does not have a sufficient interest in the determination of that application.

General provisions as to making and effect of declarations

Section 59 of the Act deals with general provisions relating to the making and effect of declarations. Subsection (1) of section 59 states that where on an application for a declaration under section 58 the truth of the proposition to be declared is proved to the satisfaction of the court, the court must make the declaration unless to do so would be manifestly contrary to public policy.

Subsection (2) states that ay declaration under section 58 binds her majesty and all other persons.

Subsection (3) states that the court, on the dismissal of an application for a declaration under section 58, may not make any declaration for which an application has not been made.

Subsection (4) states that no declaration which may be applied for under section 58 may be made otherwise than under section 58 by any court.

Subsection (5) states that no declaration may be made by any court, whether under section 58 or otherwise, that a civil partnership was, at its inception void.

Subsection (6) states that nothing in this section affects the powers of any court to make a nullity order in respect of a civil partnership.

The Attorney General and proceedings for declarations

Section 60 of the Act deals with the powers of the Attorney General to intervene with an application under section 58 and also the powers of the court to refer a matter to him or her.

Supplementary provisions as to declarations

Section 61 deals with supplementary provisions relating to declarations. Subsection (1) of section 61 of the Act states that any declaration made under section 68, and any application for such a declaration, must be in the form prescribed by the rules of the court. Subsection (2) states that the rules of the court may make provision as to the information required to be given by any applicant for a declaration under section 58. The rules can also require notice of an application under section 58 to be served on the attorney general and on persons who may be affected by any declaration applied for.

Subsection (3) states that no proceedings under section 58 affect any final judgement or order already pronounced or made by any court of competent jurisdiction.

Subsection (4) states that the court hearing an application under section 58 may direct that the whole or part of any proceedings must be heard in private.

Subsection (5) states that an application for a direction under subsection (4) must be heard in private unless the court other wise directs.

General provisions under Chapter two of the Act

Sections 62 63 and 64 deal with general provisions. Section 62 deals with relief for respondents in dissolution proceedings, Section 63 deals with restrictions on making of orders affecting children (the court must consider the effects of any dissolution, nullity or separation orders on the welfare of children). Subsection (1) of section 63 states that in any proceedings for a dissolution, nullity or separation order, the court must consider:

a) whether there are any children of the family to whom this section applies, and

b) if thee are any such children, whether (in the light of the arrangements which have been, or are proposed to be, made for their upbringing and welfare) it should exercise any of its powers under the Children Act 1989 (c.41) with respect to any of them.

Subsection (2) states that, if, in the case of any child to whom this section applies, it appears to the court that-

a) the circumstances of the case require it, or are likely to require it, to exercise any of its powers under the 1989 Act with respect to any such child,

b) it is not in the position to exercise the power or (as the case may be) those powers without giving further consideration to the case, and

c) there are exceptional circumstances which make it desirable in the interests of the child that the court should give a direction under this section, it may direct that the order is not to be made final, or (in the case of a separation order) is not to be made, until the court orders otherwise.

Subsection (3) states that this section applies to:

a) any child of the family who has not reached 16 at the date when the court considers the case in accordance with the requirements of this section, and

b) any child of the family who has reached 16 at that date and in relation to whom the court directs that this section shall apply.

Section 64 deals with general rules concerning parties to proceedings under Chapter 2 of the act.

4

Property and Financial Arrangements

Part 2. Chapter 3

Property and Financial Arrangements
Section 65 of Chapter 3 of the 2004 Civil Partnerships Act deals with property and financial arrangements in relation to entitlements generally and the event of a dissolution and ending of a partnership.

Subsection (1) of section 65 applies if:

a) a civil partner contributes in money or money's worth to the improvement of real or personal property in which or in the proceeds of sale of which either or both of the civil partners has or have a beneficial interest, and

b) the contribution is of a substantial nature.

Subsection (2) states that the contributing partner is to be treated as having acquired by virtue of the contribution a share or an enlarged share (as the case may be) in the beneficial interest of such an extent:

a) as may have been then agreed, or
b) in default of such agreement, as may seem in all the circumstances just to any court before which the question of the existence or extent of the beneficial interest of either civil partners arises (whether in proceedings between them or in any other proceedings)

Subsection (3) states that subsection (2) is subject to any agreement (express or implied) between the civil partners to the contrary.

Disputes between civil partners about property

Section 66 of the Act deals with disputes about property. Subsection (1) of section 66 states that in any question between the civil partners in a civil partnership as to title to or possession of property, either civil partner may apply to the High Court or such county court as may be prescribed by rules of court.

Subsection (2) states that on such an application, the court may make such order with respect to the property as it thinks fit (including an order for the sale of the property).

Subsection (3) states that rules of the court made for the purpose of this section may confer jurisdiction on county courts whatever the situation or value of the property in dispute.

Applications under section 66 where property not in possession etc.

Section 67 deals with applications under section 66 where one or other civil partner has property which is in possession of one person only.

Subsection (1) of section 67 states that the right of a civil partner (A) to make an application under section 66 includes the right to make such an application where A claims that the other civil partner (B) has had in his possession or under his control:

a) money to which, or to a share of which, A was beneficially entitled, or

b) property (other than money) to which, or to an interest in which, A was beneficially entitled, and that either the money or other property has ceased to be in B's possession or under B's control or that A does not know whether it is still in B's possession or under B's control.

Subsection (2) states that for the purposes of subsection (1)(a) it does not matter whether A is beneficially entitled to the money or share:

a) because it represents the proceeds of the property to which, or to an interest in which, A was beneficially entitled, or
b) for any other reason.

Subsection (3) states that subsections (4) and (5) below apply if, on such an application being made, the court is satisfied that B:

a) has had in his possession or under his control money or other property as mentioned in subsection (1)(a) or (b), and
b) has not made to A, in respect of that money or other property, such payment or disposition as would have been appropriate in the circumstances.

Subsection (4) states that the power of the court to make orders under section 66 includes power to order B to pay A:

a) in a case falling within subsection (1)(a) such sum in respect of the money to which the application relates, or A's share of it, the court considers appropriate, or
b) in a case falling within subsection (1)(b), such sum in respect of the value of the property to which the application relates, or A's interest in it, as the court considers appropriate.

Subsection (5) states that if it appears to the court that there is any property which:

a) represents the whole or the part of the money or property, and
b) is property in respect of which an order could (apart from this section) have been made under section 66, the court may (either instead of or as well as making an order in accordance with subsection (4) make any order which it could (apart from this section) have made under section 66.

Subsection (6) states that any power of the court which is exercisable on an application under section 66 is exercisable in relation to an application made under that section as extended by that section.

Applications under section 66 by former civil partners

Section 68 of the Act deals with applications by former civil partners. Subsection (1) of section 68 states that this section applies where a civil partnership has been dissolved or annulled. Subsection (2) states that, subject to subsection (3) below, an application may be made under section 66 (including that section as extended by section 67) by either former civil partner despite the dissolution or annulment (and references in those sections to a civil partner are to be read accordingly).

Subsection (3) states that the application must be made within the period of 3 years beginning with the date of the dissolution or annulment.

Actions in tort between civil partners

Section 69 of the Act deals with tortuous actions between civil partners. Subsection (1) of section 69 states that this section applies if an action in tort is brought by one civil partner against the other during the subsistence of the civil partnership.

Subsection (2) states that the court may stay the proceedings if it appears:

a) that no substantial benefit would accrue to either civil partner from the continuation of the proceedings, or

b) that the question or questions in issue could more conveniently be disposed of on an application under section 66.

Subsection (3) states that without prejudice to subsection (2)(b) the court may in such an action-

a) exercise any power which could be exercised on an application under section 66, or

b) give such direction as it thinks fit for the disposal under that section of any question arising in the proceedings.

Assurance policy by civil partner for benefit of other civil partner etc.

Section 70 of the Act deals with above policies of assurance. Section 11 of the Married Women's Property Act 1882 (c.75) (money paid under policy of insurance not to form part of the estate of the insured) applies in relation to a policy of assurance:

a) effected by a civil partner on his own life, and

b) expressed to be for the benefit of his civil partner, or of his children, or of his civil partner and children, or any of them, as it applies in relation to a policy of assurance effected by a husband and expressed to be for the benefit of his wife, or of his children, or of his wife and children, or of any of them.

Wills, administration of estates and family provision

Section 71 deals with wills and estates administration and states that schedule 4 to the Act amends enactments relating to wills, administration of estates and family provisions so that they apply in civil partnerships as they apply to marriages.

Financial relief for civil partners and children of the family

Section 72 of the Act deals with financial relief during a proceedings to end a civil partnership. Subsection (1) of section 72 states that Schedule 5 to the Act makes provision for financial relief in connection with civil partnerships that corresponds to provision made for financial relief in connection with marriages by part 2 of the Matrimonial Causes Act 1973 (c.18).

Subsection (2) states that any rule of law under which any provision of Part 2 of the 1973 Act is interpreted as applying to dissolution of a marriage on the ground of presumed death is to be treated as applying (with any necessary modifications) in relation to the corresponding provision of Schedule 5.

Subsection (3) states that Schedule 6 to the Act makes provision for financial relief in connection with civil partnerships that corresponds to provision made for financial relief in connection with marriages by the Domestic Proceedings and Magistrates Court Act 1978 (c.22).

Subsection (4) Schedule 7 to the Act makes provision for financial relief in England and Wales after a civil partnership has been dissolved or annulled, or civil partners have been legally separated, in a country outside the British Islands.

5

Civil Partnership Agreements

Part 2. Chapter 4

Civil partnership agreements unenforceable

Section 73 of the Civil Partnerships Act deals with civil partnership agreements and their contractual and other nature.

Subsection (1) of section 73 states that a civil partnership agreement does not under the law of England and Wales have effect as a contract giving rise to legal rights.

Subsection (2) states that no action lies in England and Wales for breach of a civil partnership agreement, whatever the law applicable to the agreement.

Subsection (2) states that in this section and section 74 (below) 'civil partnership agreement' means an agreement between two people:

a) to register as civil partners of each other-

      (i)   in England and Wales (under this part),

      (ii)   in Scotland (in Part 3),

      (iii)   in Northern Ireland (under Part 4), or

      (iv)   outside the United Kingdom under an order in Council made under chapter 1 of Part 5 (registration at British Consulates etc, or by armed forces personnel) or

b) to enter into an overseas relationship.

Subsection (4) states that this section applies in relation to civil partnership agreements whether entered into before or after this section comes into force, but does not affect any action commenced before it comes into force.

Property where civil partnership agreement is terminated

Subsection (1) of section 74 states that section 74 applies if a civil partnership agreement is terminated. Subsection (2) states that section 65 (contributions by civil partners to property improvements) applies, in relation to any property in which either or both of the parties to the agreement had a beneficial interest while the agreement was in force, as it applies in relation to property in which a civil partner has a beneficial interest.

Subsection (3) states that sections 66 and 67 (disputes between civil partners about property) apply to any dispute between or claim by one of the parties in relation to property in which either or both had a beneficial interest while the agreement was in force, as if the parties were civil partners of each other.

Subsection (4) states that an application made under section 66 or 67 by virtue of subsection (3) must be made within 3 years of the termination of the agreement.

Subsection (5) states that a party to a civil partnership agreement who makes a gift of property to the other party on the condition (express or implied) that it is to be returned if the agreement is terminated is not prevented from recovering the property merely because of his having terminated the agreement.

6

Children

Part 2. Chapter 5

Children

Parental responsibility, children of the family and relatives

The welfare of children generally is of the utmost importance and Section 75 of the Civil Partnerships Act 2004 deals with the responsibility of civil partners to children and family following a civil partnership.

Subsection (1) of section 75 states that the Children's Act 1989 (c.41) (the 1989 Act) is amended as follows.

Subsection (2) defines the amendment, in section 4A(1)(acquisition of parental responsibility by stepparent after 'is married to' insert 'or a civil partner of'.

Subsection (3) states in section 105(1) (interpretation) for the definition of 'child of the family' (in relation to the parties to a marriage) substitute-

"child of the family", in relation to parties to a marriage, or two people who are civil partners of each other, means-

a) a child of both of them, and
b) any other child, other than a child placed with them as foster parents by a local authority or voluntary organisation, who has been treated by both of them as a child of their family".

Subsection (4) states that in the definition of "relative" in section 105(1), for "by affinity" substitute "by marriage or civil partnership".

Guardianship

Section 76 of the Act deals with guardianship of children. In section 6 of the 1989 Act (guardians: revocation and disclaimer) after subsection 3(A) insert-

"(3B) An appointment under section 5(3) or (4) (including one made in an unrevoked will or codicil) is revoked if the person appointed is the civil partner of the person who made the appointment and either-

a) an order of the court of civil jurisdiction in England and Wales dissolves or annuls the civil partnership, or
b) the civil partnership is dissolved or annulled and the dissolution or annulment is entitled to recognition in England and Wales by virtue of Chapter 3 of Part 5 of the Civil partnership Act 2004, unless a contrary intention appears by appointment.

Entitlement to apply for residence or contact order

Section 77 of the Act deals with entitlement to apply for residence or contact order. In section 10(5) of the 1989 Act (persons entitled to apply for residence or contact order) after paragraph (a) insert-

" (as) any civil partner in a civil partnership (whether or not subsisting) in relation to whom the child is a child of the family".

Financial provision for children

Section 78 of the Act deals with financial provision for children. Subsection (1) of section 78 amends Schedule 1 to the 1989 Act (financial provision for children) as follows in subsection (2).

In paragraph 2(6) (meaning of periodical payments order) after paragraph (d) insert-

" (e) Part 1 or 9 of Schedule 5 to the Civil partnership Act 2004 (financial relief in the High Court or a county court etc);

(f) Schedule 6 to the 2004 Act (financial relief in the magistrate's court etc),".

Subsection (3) states that in paragraph 15(2) (person with whom a child lives or is to live) after "husband or wife" insert "or civil partner".

Subsection (4) states for paragraph 16(2) (extended meaning of "parent") substitute-

"(2) In this Schedule, except paragraphs 2 and 15, "parent" includes-

a) any party to a marriage (whether or not subsisting) in relation to whom the child concerned is a child of the family, and
b) any civil partner in a civil partnership (whether or not subsisting) in relation to whom the child concerned is a child of the family;

and for this purpose any reference to either parent or both parents shall be read as a reference to any parent of his and to all of his parents".

Adoption
Section 79 of the Act deals with civil partnership and adoption. Subsection (1) amends the Adoption and Children Act of 2002 (c.38) as follow.

Subsection (2) states in section 21 (placement orders) in subsection (4)(c) after "child marries" insert "forms a civil partnership".

Subsection (3) states in section 47 (condition for making adoption orders) after subsection (8) insert-

"(8A) An adoption order may not be made in relation to a person who is or has been a civil partner".

Subsection (4) states in section 51 (adoption by one person), in subsection (1) after " is not married" insert "or a civil partner".
Subsection (5) states after section 51(3) insert-

"(3A) An adoption order may be made on the application of one person who has attained the age of 21 years and is a civil partner if the court is satisfied that-

a) the persons civil partner cannot be found
b) the civil partners have separated and are living apart, and the separation is likely to be permanent, or
c) the persons civil partner is by reason of ill health, whether physical or mental, incapable of making an application for an adoption order".

Subsection (6) states in section 64 (other provisions to be made by regulations) in subsection (5) for "or marriage" substitute "marriage or civil partnership".

Subsection (7) states in section 74(1) (enactments for whose purposes section 67 does not apply) for paragraph (a) substitute-

"(a) section 1 of and Schedule 1 to the Marriage Act 1949 or Schedule 1 to the Civil Partnership Act 2004 (prohibited degrees of kindred and affinity).

Subsection (8) states in section 79 (connections between the register and birth records) , in subsection (7)-

a) in paragraph (b) after "intends to be married" insert "or forms a civil partnership" and
b) for "the person whom the applicant intends to marry" substitute "the intended spouse or civil partner".

Subsection (9) states in section 81 (Adoption Contact Register: supplementary), in subsection (2) for "or marriage" substitute marriage or civil partnership".

Subsection (10) states in section 98 (pre-commencement adoptions: information), in subsection (7), in the definition of "relative" for "or marriage" substitute "marriage or civil partnership".

Subsection (11) states in section 144 (interpretation), in the definition of "relative" in subsection (1), after "by marriage" insert "or civil partnership".

Subsection (12) states in section 144(4) (meaning of "couple"), after paragraph (a) insert-

"(aa) two people who are civil partners of each other, or"

7

Miscellaneous Provisions

Part 2. Chapter 6 of the Civil Partnerships Act 2004

Miscellaneous

False statements with reference to civil partnerships
Section 80 of the Civil Partnerships Act 2004 deals with the making of false statements when entering into a civil partnership.

Subsection 1 states that a person commits an offence if:

a) for the purpose of procuring the formation of a civil partnership, or a document mentioned in subsection (2) below, he-

    (i)   makes or signs a declaration required under this Part or Part 5, or

    (ii)   gives a notice so required.

knowing that the declaration, notice or certificate is false,

b) for the purpose of a record being made in any register relating to civil partnerships, he-

    (i)   makes a statement as to any information which is required to be registered under this Part or Part 5, or

    (ii)   causes such a statement to be made,

knowing that this statement is false.

(c) he forbids the issue of a document mentioned in subsection (2)(a) or (b) by representing himself to be a person whose consent to a civil partnership between a child and another person is required under this Part or Part 5, knowing the representation to be false, or

(d) with respect to a declaration made under paragraph 5(1) of Schedule 1 he makes a statement mentioned in paragraph 6 of that Schedule which he knows to be false in a material particular.

Subsection (2) states that the documents are:

a) a civil partnership schedule or a Registrar General's licence under chapter 1;
b) a document required by an order in council under section 210 or 211 as an authority for two people to register as civil partners of each other,
c) a certificate of no impediment under s240.

Subsection (3) states a person guilty of an offence under subsection (1) is liable-

a) on conviction on indictment, to imprisonment for a term not exceeding 7 years or to a fine or both,
b) on summary conviction, to a fine not exceeding the statutory maximum.

Subsection (4) states that the Perjury Act 1911 (c.6) has effect as if this section were contained within it.

Housing and Tenancies

Section 81 deals with housing and tenancies. Schedule 8 to the Act (see appendix) amends certain enactments relating to housing and tenancies.

Family homes and Domestic violence

Section 82 deals with family homes and domestic violence. Schedule 9 (see appendix) amends Part 4 of the Family Law Act 1996 (c.27) and related enactments so that they apply in relation to civil partnerships as they apply in relation to marriages.

Fatal accident claims

Section 83 deals with fatal accident claims. Subsection (1) of section 83 amends the Fatal Accidents Act 1976 (c.30) as follows. Subsection (2) provides the amendment. In section 1(3) (meaning of "dependant" for purposes of right of action for wrongful action causing death) after paragraph (a) insert-

"(aa) the civil partner or former civil partner of the deceased".

Subsection (3) states in paragraph (b)(iii) of section 1(3) after "wife" insert "or civil partner".

Subsection (4) states after paragraph (f) of section 1(3) insert-

"(fa) any person (not being a child of the deceased) who, in the case of any civil partnership in which the deceased was at any time a civil partner, was treated by the deceased as a child of the family in relation to that civil partnership".

Subsection (5) states after section 1(4) insert-

"(4A) The reference to the former civil partner of the deceased in subsection (3)(aa) above includes a reference to a person whose civil partnership with the deceased has been annulled as well as a person whose civil partnership with the deceased has been dissolved".

Subsection 6 states in section 1(5)(a), for "by affinity" substitute "by marriage or civil partnership".

Subsection (7) states in section 1A(2) (persons for whose benefit claim for bereavement damages may be made)-

a) in paragraph (a) after "wife or husband" insert "or civil partner" and
b) in paragraph (b), after "was never married" insert "or a civil partner".

Evidence

Section 84 deals with the giving of evidence. Subsection (1) of section 84 states that any enactment or rule of law relating to the giving of evidence by a spouse applies in relation to a civil partner as it applies in relation to a spouse. Subsection (2) states that subsection (1) is subject to any specific amendment made by or under this Act which relates to the giving of evidence by a civil partner.

Subsection (3) states that for the avoidance of doubt, in any such amendment reference to a persons civil partner do not include a former civil partner.

Subsection (4) states that references to subsections (1) and (2) to giving evidence are to giving evidence in any way (whether by supplying information, making discovery, producing documents or otherwise.)

Subsection (5) states that any rule of law:

a) which is preserved by section 7(3) of the Civil Evidence Act 1995 (c.38) or section 118(1) of the Criminal Justice Act 2003 (c.44) and

b) under which in any proceedings evidence of reputation or family tradition is admissible for the purpose of proving or disproving the existence of a marriage,

is to be treated as applying in an equivalent way for the purpose of proving or disproving the existence of a civil partnership.

8

Part 5. Civil Partnerships Formed or Dissolved Abroad

Part 5. Chapter 1 of the Civil Partnerships Act 2004

Registration outside U.K. under Order in Council.

Registration at British Consulates etc.
Section 210 of the CPA 2004 deals with registration at British Consulates and other matters.

Subsection (1) of section 210 states that Her Majesty may by Order in Council make provision for two people to register as civil partners of each other:

    a) in prescribed countries or territories outside the United Kingdom, and

    b) in the presence of a prescribed officer of Her Majesty's Diplomatic Service

in cases where the officer is satisfied that the conditions in subsection (2) below are met.

Subsection (2) lays out those conditions as follows:

    a) at least one of the proposed civil partners is a United Kingdom national,

    b) the proposed civil partners would have been eligible to register as civil partners of each other in such part of the United Kingdom as is determined in accordance with the order,

c) the authorities of the countries or territory in which it is proposed that they register as civil partners will not object to the registration, and

d) insufficient facilities exist for them to enter into an overseas relationship under the law of that country or territory.

Subsection (3) states that an officer is not required to allow two people to register as civil partners of each other if in his opinion the formation of a civil partnership between them would be inconsistent with international law or the comity of nations.

Subsection (4) states that an Order in Council under this section may make provision for appeals against a refusal, in reliance on subsection (3), to allow two people to register as civil partners of each other.

Subsection (5) states that an Order in Council under this section may provide that two people who register as civil partners of each other under such an order are to be treated for the purposes of sections 221(1)(c)(i) and(2)(c)(i),222©,224(b),225(c)(i) and (3)(c)(i),229(c)(i) and (2)(c)(i),230(c) and 232(b)(i) of the Presumption of Death (Scotland) Act 1977 (c.27) as if they had done so in the part of the United Kingdom determined as mentioned in subsection (2)(b).

Registration by armed forces personnel

Section 211 of the Act deals with armed forces personnel. Subsection (1) of section 211 states that her majesty may by Order in Council make provision for two people to register as civil partners of each other:

a) in prescribed countries or territories outside the United Kingdom, and

b) in the presence of an officer appointed by virtue of the Registration of Births, Deaths and marriages (Special Provisions) Act 1957 (c.58).

in cases where the officer is satisfied that the conditions in subsection (2) below are met. Subsection (2) lays out those conditions:

a) at least one of the proposed civil partners-

   (i)   is a member of a part of Her Majesty's forces serving in the country or territory,

   (ii)   is employed in the country or territory in such other capacity as may be prescribed, or

   (iii) is a child of a person falling within sub-paragraph (i) or (ii) and has his home with that person in that country or territory,

(b) the proposed civil partners would have been eligible to register as civil partners of each other in such part of the United Kingdom as is determined in accordance with the Order, and

(c) such other requirements as may be prescribed are complied with.

Subsection (3) states that in determining for the purposes of subsection (2) whether one person is the child of another, a person who is or was treated by another as a child of the family in relation to:

a) a marriage to which the other is or was a party, or
b) a civil partnership in which the other is or was a civil partner

is to be regarded as the other's child.

Subsection (4) states that an Order in Council under this section may provide that two people who register as civil partners of each other under such an order are to be treated for the purposes of section 221(1)(c)(i) and (2)(c)(i),222 (c), 224(b) 225(1) (c) (i) 229(1)(c) (i) and (2) (c) (i) 230 (c) and 232 (b) and section 1 (3)(c)(i) of the Presumption of Death (Scotland) Act 1977 (c.27) as if they had done so in the part of the United Kingdom determined in accordance with subsection (2)(b).

Subsection 5 states that any references made in this section:

a) to a country or territory outside the United Kingdom,
b) to forces serving in such a country or territory, and
c) to persons employed in such a country or territory,

include references to ships which are for the time being in the waters of a country or territory outside the United Kingdom, to forces serving in any such ship and to persons employed in any such ship.

9

Overseas relationships treated as civil partnerships

Part 5. Chapter 2

Meaning of overseas relationship
Section 212 of the Act deals further with overseas relationships. Subsection (1) states that for the purposes of this Act an overseas relationship is a relationship which:

a) is either a specified relationship or a relationship which meets the general conditions, and
b) is registered (whether before or after the passing of this Act) with a responsible authority in a country or territory outside the United Kingdom, by two people-

    (i)   who under the relevant law are of the same sex at the time when they do so, and

    (ii)   neither of whom is already a civil partner or lawfully married.

Subsection (2) states that in this chapter, "the relevant law" means the law of the country or territory where the relationship is registered (including its rules of private international law).

Specified relationships
Section 213 subsection (1) deals with specified relationships, as defined by Schedule 20 to the Act. Subsection (2) states that the Secretary of State may by an order amend Schedule 20 by:

a) adding a relationship,

b) amending the description of a relationship, and
c) omitting a relationship.

Subsection (3) states that no order may be made under this section without the consent of the Scottish Ministers and the Department of Finance and Personnel.

Subsection (4) states that the power to make an order under this section is excercisable by statutory instrument.

Subsection (5) states that an order which contains any provision (whether alone or with other provisions) amending Schedule 20 by-

a) amending the description of a relationship, or
b) omitting a relationship,

may not be made unless a draft of the statutory instrument containing the order is laid before, and approved by a resolution of, each house of parliament.

The general conditions

Section 214 deals with general conditions and civil partnerships abroad. The general conditions are that, under the relevant law:

a) the relationship may not be entered into if either of the parties is already a party to a relationship of that kind or lawfully married,
b) the relationship is of an indeterminate duration, and
c) the effect of entering into it is that the parties are-

(i) treated as a couple either generally or for specified purposes, or
(ii) treated as married.

Overseas relationships treated as civil partnerships: the general rule

Section 215 deals with overseas relationships which are treated as civil partnerships. Subsection (10 states that two people are to be treated as having formed a civil partnership as a result of having registered an overseas relationship if, under the relevant law, they:

a) had capacity to enter into the relationship, and
b) met all requirements necessary to ensure the formal validity of the relationship.

Subsection (2) states that subject to subsection (3) below, the time when they are to be treated as having formed the civil partnership is the time when the overseas relationship is registered (under the relevant law) as having been entered into.

Subsection (3) states that if the overseas relationship is registered (under the relevant law) as having been entered into before this section comes into force, the time when they are treated as having formed a civil partnership is the time when this section comes into force.

Subsection (4) states that if:

a) before this section comes into force, a dissolution or annulment of the overseas relationship was obtained outside the United Kingdom, and
b) the dissolution or annulment would be recognised under Chapter 3 if the overseas relationship had been treated as a civil partnership at the time of the dissolution or annulment,

subsection (3) does not apply and subsections (1) and (2) have effect subject to subsection (5).

Subsection (5) states that the overseas relationship is not to be treated as having been a civil partnership for the purposes of any provisions except:

a) Schedules 7, 11 and 17 (financial relief in United Kingdom after dissolution or annulment obtained outside the United Kingdom);

b) Such provisions as are specified (with or without modifications) in an order under s 259;
c) Chapter 3 (so far as necessary for the purposes of paragraphs (a) and (b)).

Subsection (6) that this section is subject to sections 216, 217 and 218.

The same sex requirement

Section 216 deals with the same sex requirement. Subsection (1) states that two people are not to be treated as having formed a civil partnership as a result of having registered an overseas relationship if, at the critical time, they were not of the same sex under United Kingdom law.

Subsection (2) states that if a full gender recognition certificate is issued under the 2004 Act to a person who has registered an overseas relationship which is within subsection (4) below after the issue of the certificate the relationship is no longer prevented from being treated as a civil partnership on the ground that, at the critical time, the parties were not of the same sex.

Subsection (3) states that, however, subsection (2) does not apply to an overseas relationship which is within subsection (4) below if either of the parties has formed a subsequent civil partnership or lawful marriage.

Subsection (4) states that an overseas relationship is within this section if (and only if) at the time mentioned in section 215(2)-

a) one of the parties ("A") was regarded under the relevant law as having changed gender (but was not regarded under United Kingdom law as having done so), and
b) the other party was (under United Kingdom law) of the gender to which A had changed under the relevant law.

Subsection (5) states that, in this section-

"the critical time" means the time determined in accordance with section 215(2) or (as the case may be) (3);

"the 2004 Act" means the Gender Recognition Act 2004 (c.7);
"United Kingdom law" means any enactment or rule of law applying in England and Wales, Scotland and Northern Ireland.

Subsection (6) states that nothing in this section prevents the exercise of any enforceable community right.

Persons domiciled in a part of the United Kingdom
Section 217 deals with domicile in a part of the United Kingdom. Subsection 1 (2) of section 217 applies if an overseas relationship has been registered by a person who was at the time mentioned in section 215 (2) domiciled in England and Wales.

Subsection (2) states that the two people concerned are not to be treated as having formed a civil partnership if, at the time mentioned in section 215 (2)-

a) either of them was under 16, or
b) they would have been within prohibited degrees of relationship under Part 1 of schedule 1 if they had been registering as civil partners of each other in England and Wales.

Subsection (3) states that subsection (4) applies if an overseas relationship has been registered by a person who at the time mentioned in section 215 (2) was domiciled in Scotland.

Subsection (4) states that the two people concerned are not to be treated as having formed a civil partnership if, at the time mentioned in section 215 (2), they were not eligible by virtue of paragraph (b), (c) or (e) of section 86(1) to register in Scotland as civil partners of each other.

Subsection (5) states that subsection (6) applies if an overseas relationship has been registered by a person who at the time mentioned in section 215(2) was domiciled in Northern Ireland.

Subsection (6) states that the two people concerned are not to be treated as having formed a civil partnership if, at the time mentioned in s125 (2)-

a) either of them was under 16,or
b) b) they would have been within prohibited degrees of relationship under Schedule 12 if they had been registering as civil partners of each other in Northern Ireland.

The public policy exception

Section 218 states that two people are not to be treated as having formed a civil partnership as a result of having entered into an overseas relationship if it would be manifestly contrary to public policy to recognise the capacity under the relevant law, of one or both of them to enter into the relationship.

10

Dissolution etc: Jurisdiction and recognition

Part 5. Chapter 3

Power to make provision corresponding to EC Regulation 2201/2003.

Section 219 deals with jurisdiction of courts in England and Wales. Subsection (1) of section 219 states that the Lord Chancellor may by regulations make provision:

a) as to the jurisdiction of courts in England and Wales or Northern Ireland in proceedings for the dissolution or annulment of a civil partnership or for legal separation of the civil partners in cases where a civil partner-

    (i)   is or has been habitually resident in a member state,

    (ii)   is a national of a member state, or

    (iii)   is domiciled in a part of the United Kingdom or the Republic of Ireland, and

b) as to the recognition in England and Wales or Northern Ireland of any judgement of a court or another member state which orders the dissolution or annulment of a civil partnership or the legal separation of the legal partners.

Subsection (2) states that the Scottish Ministers may by regulations make provision:

a) as to the jurisdiction of courts in Scotland in proceedings for the dissolution or annulment of a civil partnership or for legal separation of the civil partners in such cases as are mentioned in subsection (1)(a), and

b) as to the recognition in Scotland of any such judgement as is mentioned in subsection (1)(b).

Subsection (3) states that the regulations may in particular make provision corresponding to that made by council regulation (EC) No 2201/2003 of 27th November 2003 in relation to jurisdiction and the recognition and enforcement of judgements in matrimonial matters.

Subsection (4) states that the regulations may provide that for the purposes of this part and the regulations "member state" means:

a) all member states with the exception of such member states as are specified in the regulations, or

b) such member states as are specified in the regulations.

Subsection (5) states that the regulations may make provision under subsections (1)(b) and (2)(b) which applies even if the date of the dissolution, annulment or legal separation is earlier than the date on which this section comes into force.

Subsection (6) states that regulations under subsection (1) are to be made by statutory instrument and may only be made if a draft has been laid before and approved by resolution of each house of parliament.

Subsection (7) states that regulations under subsection (2) are to be made by statutory instrument and may only be made if a draft has been laid before and approved by resolution of the Scottish Parliament.

Subsection (8) states that, in this part "section 219 regulations" means regulations made under this section.

Jurisdiction of courts in England and Wales

Meaning of "the court"

Section 220 of the Act deals with meaning of "the court". In sections 221 to 224 "the court" means-

a) the High Court, or
b) if a county court has jurisdiction by virtue of part 5 of the Matrimonial and Family Proceedings Act 1984 (c.42), a county court.

Proceedings for dissolution, separation or nullity order

Section 221 deals with proceedings for dissolution, separation or nullity orders. Subsection (1) states that the court has jurisdiction to entertain proceedings for a dissolution order or a separation order if (and only if)-

a) the court has jurisdiction under section 219 regulations,
b) no court has, or is recognised as having, jurisdiction under section 219 regulations and either civil partner is domiciled in England and Wales on the date when the proceedings are begun, or
c) the following conditions are met-

    (i)   the two people concerned registered as civil partners of each other in England and Wales,
    (ii)   no court has, or is recognised as having, jurisdiction under section 219 regulations, and
    (iii)   it appears to the court to be in the interests of justice to assume jurisdiction in the case.

(2) Subsection (2) states that the court has jurisdiction to entertain proceedings for a nullity order if (and only if)-

a) the court has jurisdiction under section 219 regulations,
b) no court has, or is recognised as having, jurisdiction under section 219 regulations and either civil partner-

(i)   is domiciled in England and Wales on the date when the proceedings are begun, or

(ii)   died before that date and either was at death domiciled in England and Wales or had been habitually resident in England and Wales throughout the period of 1 year ending at the date of death, or

c) the following conditions are met-

(i)   the two people concerned registered as civil partners of each other in England and Wales,

(ii)   no court has, or is recognised as having, jurisdiction under section 219 regulations, and

(iii) it appears in the courts to be in the interests of justice to assume jurisdiction in the case.

Subsection (3) states that at any time when proceedings are pending in respect of which the court has jurisdiction by virtue of subsection (1) or (2) (or this subsection), the court also has jurisdiction to entertain other proceedings, in respect of the same civil partnership, for a dissolution, separation or nullity order, even though that jurisdiction would not be exercisable under subsection (1) or (2).

Proceedings for presumption of death order

Section 222 deals with proceedings for a presumption of death order. The court has jurisdiction to entertain proceedings for a presumption of death order if (and only if)-

a) the applicant is domiciled in England and Wales on the date when proceedings are begun,

b) the applicant was habitually resident in England and Wales throughout the period of 1 year ending with that date, or

c) the two people concerned registered as civil partners of each other in England and Wales and it appears to the court to be in the interests of justice to assume jurisdiction in the case.

Proceedings for dissolution, nullity or separation order: supplementary

Section 223 deals with supplementary provisions. Subsection (1) of section 223 states that the rules of the court make provision in relation to civil partnerships corresponding to the provision made in relation to marriages by Schedule 1 to the Domicile and Matrimonial Proceedings Act 1973 (c.45).

Subsection (2) states that the rules may in particular make provisions-

a) for the provision of information by applicants and respondents in proceedings for dissolution, nullity or separation orders where proceedings relating to the same civil partnership are continuing in another jurisdiction, and
b) for proceedings before the court to be stayed by the court where there are concurrent proceedings elsewhere in respect of the same civil partnership.

Applications for declaration as to validity etc.

Section 224 deals with applications for declarations as to validity and other provisions. The court has jurisdiction to entertain an application under section 58 if (and only if)-

a) either of the civil partners in the civil partnership to which the application relates-

   (i) is domiciled in England and Wales on the date of the application,

   (ii) has been habitually resident in England and Wales throughout the period of 1 year ending with that date, or

   (iii) died before that date and either was at the death domiciled in England and Wales or had been habitually resident in England and Wales throughout the period of 1 year ending with the date of death, or

b) the two people concerned registered as civil partners of each other in England and Wales and it appears to the court to be in the interests of justice to assume jurisdiction in the case.

Jurisdiction of Scottish Courts

Section 225 of the Act deals with jurisdiction of the Scottish Courts. Subsection (1) of section 225 states that the court of session has jurisdiction to entertain an action for the dissolution of a civil partnership or for separation of civil partners if (and only if)-

a) the court has jurisdiction under section 219 regulations
b) no court has, or is recognised as having, jurisdiction under section 219 regulations and either civil partner is domiciled in Scotland on the date when the proceedings are begun, or
c) the following conditions are met-

(i)   the two people concerned registered as civil partners of each other in Scotland
(ii)   no court has, or is recognised as having, jurisdiction under s 129 regulations, and
(iii)   it appears to the courts to be in the interests of justice to assume jurisdiction in the case.

Subsection (2) states that the sheriff has jurisdiction to entertain an action for the dissolution of a civil partnership or for separation of civil partners if (and only if) the requirements of paragraph (a) or (b) of subsection (1) are met and either civil partner-

a) was resident in the sherrifdom for a period of 40 days ending with the date when the action is begun, or
b) had been resident in the sherrifdom for a period of not less than 40 days ending not more than 40 days before that date and has no known residence in Scotland at that date.

Subsection 93) states that the Court of Session has jurisdiction to entertain an action for declarator of nullity of a civil partnership if (and only if)-

a) the court has jurisdiction under section 219 regulations,
b) no court has, or is recognised as having, jurisdiction under section 219 regulations and either of the ostensible civil partners-

    (i) is domiciled in Scotland on the date when the proceedings are begun, or

    (ii) died before that date and was either at death domiciled in Scotland or had been habitually resident in Scotland throughout the period of 1 year ending with the date of death, or

c) the following conditions are met-

    (i) the two people concerned registered as civil partners of each other in Scotland,

    (ii) no court has, or is recognised as having, jurisdiction under s 219 regulations, and

    (iii) it appears to the court to be in the interests of justice to assume jurisdiction in the case.

Subsection (4) states that any time when proceedings are pending in respect of which a court has jurisdiction by virtue of any of subsections (1) to (3) (or this subsection) it also has jurisdiction to entertain other proceedings, in respect of the same civil partnership (or ostensible civil partnership) for dissolution, separation or (but only where the court is court of session) declarator of nullity, even though that jurisdiction would not be exercisable under any subsections (1) to (3).

Sisting of proceedings

Section 226 deals with sisting of proceedings in Scotland. Subsection (1) of section 226 states that rules of court may make provision in relation to civil partnerships corresponding to the provision made in relation to marriages by Schedule 3 to the Domicile and Matrimonial Proceedings Act 1973 (c.45) (sisting of Scottish consitorial actions).

Subsection (2) states that the rules in particular make provision-

a) for the provision of information by the pursuer and by any other person who has entered appearance in an action where proceedings relating to the same civil partnership (or ostensible civil partnership) are continuing in another jurisdiction, and

b) for an action to be sisted where thee are concurrent proceedings elsewhere in respect of the same civil partnership (or ostensible civil partnership).

Scottish ancillary and collateral orders

Section 227 deals with Scottish ancillary and collateral orders. Subsection (1) of section 227 states that this section applies where after the commencement of this Act an application is competently made to the Court of Session or the sheriff for the making, or the variation or recall, of an order which is ancillary or collateral to an action for-

a) the dissolution of a civil partnership,
b) the separation of civil partners, or
c) declarator of nullity of a civil partnership.

Subsection (2) states that the section applies whether the application is made in the same proceedings or in other proceedings and whether it is made before or after the pronouncement of a final decree in the action.

Subsection (3) states that if the court has or, as the case may be, had jurisdiction to entertain the action, it has jurisdiction to entertain the action unless,

a) jurisdiction to entertain the action was under s129 regulations, and
b) to make, vary or recall the order to which the application relates would contravene the regulations.

Subsection (4) states that where the Court of Session has jurisdiction by virtue of this section to entertain an application for the variation or recall, as respects any person, of an order made by it and the order is one to which section 8 (variation and recall by the sheriff of certain orders made by the court of session) of the Law Reform (Miscellaneous Provisions) (Scotland) Act 1966 (c.19) applies, then for the purposes of any application under that section for the variation or recall of the order in so far as it relates to the person, the sheriff (as defined in that section) has jurisdiction to exercise the power conferred on him by that section.

Subsection (5) states that the reference in subsection (1) to an order which is ancillary or collateral is to an order relating to children, aliment, financial provision or expenses.

Jurisdiction of courts in Northern Ireland

Section 228 deals with the jurisdiction of courts in Northern Ireland and defines the meaning of "courts". In sections 229 to 232 "the court" has the meaning given by section 188.

Proceedings for dissolution, separation or nullity order

Section 229 deals with proceedings for dissolution, separation or nullity order in Northern Ireland. Subsection (1) of section 229 states that the court has jurisdiction to entertain proceedings for a dissolution order or a separation order if (and only if)-

a) the court has jurisdiction under s 219 regulations,

b) no court has, or is recognised as having, jurisdiction under section 219 regulations and either civil partner is domiciled in Northern Ireland on the date when the proceedings are begun, or

c) the following conditions are met-

   (i) the two people concerned registered as civil partners of each other in Northern Ireland,

   (ii) no court has, or is recognised as having, jurisdiction under s 219 regulations, and

   (iii) it appears to the court to be in the interests if justice to assume jurisdiction in the case.

Subsection (2) states that the court has jurisdiction to entertain proceedings for a nullity order if (and only if)-

a)   the court has jurisdiction under s 219 regulations,
b)   no court has, or is recognised as having, jurisdiction under s 219 regulations and either civil partner-

(i)   is domiciled in Northern Ireland on the date when the proceedings are begun, or

(ii)   died before that date and was either at date domiciled in Northern Ireland or had been habitually resident in Northern Ireland throughout the period of 1 year ending with the date of death, or

c)   the following conditions are met-

(i)   the two people concerned registered as civil partners of each other in Northern Ireland,

(ii)   no court has, or is recognised as having, jurisdiction under s 219 regulations, and

(iii)   it appears to the court to be in the interests of justice to assume jurisdiction in the case.

Subsection (3) states that at any time when proceedings are pending in respect of which the court has jurisdiction by virtue of subsection (1) or (2) (or this subsection) the court also has jurisdiction to entertain other proceedings, in respect of the same civil partnership, for a dissolution, separation or nullity order, even though that jurisdiction would not be exercisable under subsection (1) or (2).

Proceedings for presumption of death order

Section 230 deals with proceedings for a presumption of death order in Northern Ireland. The High Court has jurisdiction to entertain proceedings for a presumption of death order if (and only if)-

a) the applicant is domiciled in Northern Ireland on the date when the proceedings are begun,
b) the applicant was habitually resident in Northern Ireland throughout the period of 1 year ending with that date, or
c) the two people concerned registered as civil partners of each other in Northern Ireland and it appears to the high court to be in the interests of justice to assume jurisdiction in the case.

Proceedings for dissolution, nullity or separation order: supplementary

Section 231 deals with proceedings for dissolution, nullity or separation orders, supplementary provisions. Subsection (1) states that the rules of the court may make provisions in relation to civil partnerships corresponding to the provision made in relation to marriages by Schedule 1 to the Matrimonial Causes (Northern Ireland) order 1971 (S.1 1978/1045 (N.I. 15)).

Subsection (2) states that the rules in particular make provision-

a) for the provision of information by applicants and respondents in proceedings for dissolution, nullity or separation orders where proceedings relating to the same civil partnership are continuing in another jurisdiction, and
b) for proceedings before the court to be stayed by the court where there are concurrent proceedings elsewhere in respect of the same civil partnership.

Applications for declarations as to validity etc.

Section 232 deals with applications for declarations as to validity etc in Northern Ireland. The court has jurisdiction to entertain an application under section 181 if (and only if)-

a) either of the civil partners in the civil partnership to which the application relates-

(i) is domiciled in Northern Ireland on the date of the application,

103

(ii)   has been habitually resident in Northern Ireland throughout the period of 1 year ending with that date, or

(iii)   died before that date and either was at death domiciled in Northern Ireland or had been habitually resident in Northern Ireland throughout the period of 1 year ending with the date of death, or

b)   the two people concerned registered as civil partners of each other in Northern Ireland and it appears to the court to be in the interests of justice to assume jurisdiction in the case.

Recognition of dissolution, annulment and separation

Effect of dissolution, annulment or separation obtained in the UK

Section 233 deals with the effect of dissolution, annulment or separation obtained in the UK. Subsection (1) of section 233 states that no dissolution or annulment of a civil partnership obtained in one part of the United Kingdom is effective in any part of the United Kingdom unless obtained from a court of civil jurisdiction.

Subsection (2) states that subject to subsections (3) and (4) the validity of a dissolution or annulment of a civil partnership or a legal separation of civil partners which has been obtained from a court of civil jurisdiction in one part of the United Kingdom is to be recognised throughout the United Kingdom.

Subsection (3) states that recognition of the validity of a dissolution, annulment or legal separation obtained from a court of civil jurisdiction in one part of the United Kingdom may be refused in any part if the dissolution, annulment or separation was obtained at a time when it was irreconcilable with a decision determining the question of substance or validity of the civil partnership-

a)   previously given by a court of civil jurisdiction in the other part, or

b) previously given by a court elsewhere and recognised or entitled to be recognised in the other part.

Subsection (4) states that the recognition of validity of a dissolution or legal separation obtained from a court of civil jurisdiction in one part of the United Kingdom may be refused in any other part of the dissolution or separation was obtained at a time when, according to the law of the other part, there was no subsisting civil partnership.

Recognition in the U.K of overseas dissolution, annulment or separation

Section 234 deals with the recognition in the United Kingdom of an annulment, dissolution or separation carried out overseas. Subsection (1) of section 234 states that, subject to subsection (2), the validity of an overseas dissolution, annulment or legal separation is to be recognised in the United Kingdom if, and only if, it is entitled to recognition by virtue of sections 235 to 237.

Subsection (2) states that this section and sections 235 and 237 do not apply to an overseas dissolution, or annulment or a civil partnership or a legal separation as regards which provision as to which recognition is made by section 219 regulations.

Subsection (3) states that for the purposes of subsections (1) and (2) and sections 235 to 237, an overseas dissolution, annulment or legal separation is a dissolution or annulment of a civil partnership or a legal separation of civil partners which has been obtained outside the United kingdom (whether before or after this section comes into force).

Grounds for recognition

Section 235 deals with grounds for recognition. Subsection (1) of section 235 states that the validity of an overseas dissolution, annulment or legal separation obtained by means of proceedings is to be recognised if-

a) the dissolution, annulment or legal separation is effective under the law of the country in which it was obtained, and

b) at the relevant date either civil partner-

    (i) was habitually resident in the country in which the dissolution, annulment or legal separation was obtained,

    (ii) was domiciled in that country, or

    (iii) was a national of that country.

Subsection (2) states that the validity of an overseas dissolution, annulment or legal separation obtained otherwise than by means of proceedings is to be recognised if-

a) the dissolution, annulment or legal separation is effective under the law of the country in which it was obtained,

b) at the relevant date-

    (i) each civil partner was domiciled in that country, or

    (ii) either civil partner was domiciled in that country and the other was domiciled in a country under whose law the dissolution annulment or legal separation is recognised as valid, and

c) neither civil partner was habitually resident in the United Kingdom throughout the period of 1 year immediately preceding that date.

Subsection (3) in this section, the "relevant date" means-

a) in the case of an overseas dissolution, annulment or legal separation obtained by means of proceedings, the date of commencement of proceedings;

b) in the case of an overseas dissolution, annulment or legal separation obtained other wise than by means of proceedings, the date on which it was obtained.

Subsection (4) states that where in the case of an overseas annulment the relevant date fell after the death of either civil partner, any reference in subsection (1) or (2) to that date is to be read in relation to that civil partner as a reference to the date of death.

Refusal of recognition

Section 236 deals with refusal of recognition of the validity of overseas dissolutions, annulments or legal separations. Subsection (1) of section 236 states that recognition of the validity of an overseas dissolution, annulment or legal separation may be refused in any part of the United Kingdom if the dissolution, annulment or separation was obtained at a time when it was irreconcilable with a decision determining the question of the subsistence or validity of the civil partnership-

a) previously given by a court of civil jurisdiction in that part of the United Kingdom, or
b) previously given by a court elsewhere and recognised or entitled to be recognised in that part of the United Kingdom.

Subsection (2) states that recognition of the validity of an overseas dissolution or legal separation may be refused in any part of the United kingdom if the dissolution or separation was obtained at a time when, according to the law of that part of the United Kingdom, there was no subsisting civil partnership.

Subsection (3) states that recognition of the validity of an overseas dissolution, annulment or legal separation may be refused if-

a) in the case of a dissolution, annulment or legal separation obtained by means of proceedings, it was obtained-

   (i) without such steps having been taken for giving notice of the proceedings to a civil partner as, having regard to the nature of the proceedings and all the circumstances, should have reasonably been taken, or

(ii)   without a civil partner having been given (for any reason other than lack of notice) such opportunity to take part in the proceedings as, having regard to those matters, he should have reasonably been given, or

b) in the case of a dissolution, annulment or legal separation obtained otherwise than by means of proceedings-

(i)   there is no official document certifying that the dissolution, annulment or legal separation is effective under the law of the country in which it was obtained, or

(ii)   where either civil partner was domiciled in another country at the relevant date, there is no official document certifying that the dissolution, annulment or legal separation is recognised as valid under the law of that other country, or

c) in either case, recognition that the dissolution, annulment or legal separation would be manifestly contrary to public policy.

Subsection (4) states that, in this section-

"official" in relation to a document certifying that a dissolution, annulment or legal separation is effective, or is recognised as valid, under the law of any country, means issued by a person or body appointed or recognised for the purpose under that law;

"the relevant date" has the same meaning as in section 235.

Supplementary provisions relating to recognition of dissolution etc.

Section 237 deals with supplementary provisions. Subsection (1) of section 237 states that for the purposes of section 235 and 236, a civil partner is to be treated as domiciled in a country if he was domiciled in that country-

a) according to the law of that country in family matters, or
b) according to the law of the part of the United kingdom in which the question of recognition arises.

Subsection (2) states that the Lord Chancellor or the Scottish Ministers may by regulations make provision-

a) applying sections 235 and 236 and subsection 91) with modifications in relation to any country whose territories have different systems of law in force in matters of dissolution, annulment or legal separation;
b) applying sections 235 and 236 with modifications in relation to-

    (i) an overseas dissolution, annulment or legal separation in the case of an overseas relationship (or an apparent or alleged overseas relationship);

    (ii) any case where a civil partner is domiciled in a country or territory whose law does not recognise legal relationships between two people of the same sex;

c) with respect to recognition of the validity of an overseas dissolution, annulment or legal separation in cases where there are cross-proceedings;
d) with respect to cases where a legal separation is converted under the law of the country or territory in which it is obtained into a dissolution which is effective under the law of that country or territory;
e) with respect to proof of findings of fact made in proceedings in any country or territory outside the United Kingdom.

Subsection (3) states that the power to make regulations under subsection (2) is exercisable by statutory instrument.

Subsection (4) states that a statutory instrument containing such regulations-

a) if made by the Lord Chancellor, is subject to annulment in pursuance of a resolution of either House of Parliament;

b) if made by the Scottish Ministers, is subject to annulment in pursuance of a resolution of the Scottish Parliament.

Subsection (5) states that in this section (except subsection (4) and sections 233 to 236 and 238-

"annulment" includes any order annulling a civil partnership however expressed;

"part of the United Kingdom" means England and Wales, Scotland or Northern Ireland;

"proceedings" means judicial or other proceedings.

Subsection (6) states that nothing in this Chapter is to be read as requiring the recognition of any finding of fault made in proceedings for dissolution, annulment or legal separation or of any maintenance, custody or other ancillary order made in any such proceedings.

Non-recognition elsewhere of dissolution or annulment

Section 238 deals with non-recognition elsewhere of dissolution or annulment. Subsection (1) of section 238 states that this section applies where, in any part of the United Kingdom-

a) a dissolution or annulment of a civil partnership has been granted by a court of civil jurisdiction, or

b) the validity of a dissolution or annulment of a civil partnership is recognised by virtue of this chapter.

Subsection (2) states that the fact that the dissolution or annulment would not be recognised outside the United Kingdom does not-

a) preclude either party from forming a subsequent civil partnership or marriage in that part of the United Kingdom, or

b) cause the subsequent civil partnership or marriage of either party (wherever it takes place) to be treated as invalid in that part.

11

Miscellaneous and supplementary

Chapter 4. Part 5

Commanding officers certificates for part two purposes

Section 239 deals with the issue of commanding officers certificates. Subsection (1) of section 239 states that Her Majesty may by order in Council make provision in relation to cases where-

a) two people wish to register as civil partners of each other in England and Wales (under Chapter 1 of part 2), and

b) one of them (A) is a member of Her Majesty's forces serving outside the United Kingdom and the other is resident in England and Wales,

for the issue by A's commanding officer to A of a certificate of no impediment.

Subsection (2) states that the order may provide for the issue of the certificate to be subject to the giving of such notice and the making of such declarations as may be prescribed.

Subsection (3) states that a certificate of no impediment is a certificate that no legal impediment to the formation of the civil partnership has been shown to the commanding officer issuing the certificate to exist.

Subsection (4) defines 'commanding officer'-

a) in relation to the person subject to military law, means the officer who would be that persons commanding officer for the purposes of section 82 of the Army Act 1955 (3&4 Eliz.2.c 18) if he were charged with an offence;

b) in relation to a person subject to air force law, means the officer who would be that persons commanding officer for the purposes of section 82 of the Air Force Act 1955 (3&4 Eliz.2 c.19) if he were charged with an offence;

c) in relation to a person subject to the Naval Discipline Act 1957 (c.53), means the officer in command of the ship or naval establishment to which he belongs.

Certificates of no impediment to overseas relationships

Section 240 deals with certificates of no impediment to overseas relationships. Subsection (1) of section 240 states that Her Majesty may, by order in council make provision for the issue of certificates of no impediment to-

a) United Kingdom nationals, and

b) such other persons falling within subsection (2) as may be prescribed,

who wish to enter into overseas relationships in prescribed countries or territories outside the United Kingdom with persons who are not United Kingdom nationals and who do not fall within subsection (2).

Subsection (2) states that a person falls within this subsection if under any enactment for the time being in force in any country mentioned in Schedule 3 to the British Nationality Act 1981 (c.61) (Commonwealth countries) that person is a citizen of that country.

Subsection (3) states that a certificate of no impediment is a certificate that, after proper notices have been given to, no legal impediment to the recipient entering into the overseas relationship has been shown to the person issuing the certificate to exist.

Transmission of certificates of registration of overseas relationships

Section 241 deals with transmission of certificates. Subsection (1) of section 241 states that Her Majesty may, by order in council provide-

a) for the transmission to the registrar general, by such persons or in such manner as may be prescribed, of certificates, of the certificates of the registration of overseas relationships entered into by United Kingdom nationals in prescribed countries or territories outside the United Kingdom,

b) for the Issue by the Registrar General of a certified copy of such a certificate received by him, and

c) for such certified copies to be received in evidence.

Subsection (2)"The Registrar General" means-

a) in relation to England and Wales, the Registrar General for England and Wales,

b) in relation to Scotland, The Registrar General of Births, Deaths and marriages for Scotland, and

c) in relation to Northern Ireland, The Registrar General for Northern Ireland.

Power make provision relating to certain Commonwealth forces

Section 242 deals with provisions relating to certain Commonwealth forces. Subsection (1) of section 242 states that this section applies if it appears to her majesty that any law in force in Canada, the Commonwealth of Australia or New Zealand (or in a territory of either of the former two countries) makes, in relation to forces raised there, provision similar to that made by section 211 (registration by armed forces personnel).

Subsection (2) states that Her Majesty may by Order of Council make provision for securing that the law in question has effect as part of the law of the United Kingdom.

Fees

Section 243 deals with fees. Subsection (1) of section 243 states that the power to make an order under section 34 (1) (fees) includes power to make an order prescribing fees in respect of anything which, by virtue of an Order in Council under this part, is required to be done by registration authorities in England and Wales or by or on behalf of the Registrar General for England and Wales.

Subsection (2) states that regulations made by the Registrar General of Births, Deaths and Marriages for Scotland may prescribe fees in respect of anything which, by virtue of an Order in Council under this part, is required to be done by him or on his behalf.

Subsection (3) states that subsections (3) and (4) of section 126 apply to regulations made under subsection (2) as they apply to regulations under Part 3.

Subsection (4) states that the power to make an order under section 157(1) includes power to make an order prescribing fees in respect of anything which, by virtue of an Order in Council under this Part, is required to be done by or on behalf of the Registrar General for Northern Ireland.

Orders in Council: supplementary

Section 244 deals with supplementary provisions. Subsection (1) of section 244 states that an Order in Council under section 210,211,239,240,241 or 242 may make-

a)   different provision for different cases, and
b)   such supplementary, incidental, consequential, transitional, transitory or saving provision as appears to Her Majesty to be appropriate.

Subsection (2) states that the provision that may be made by virtue of subsection (1)(b) includes in particular provision corresponding to or applying with modifications any provision made by or under-

a) this act, or
b) any act relating to marriage outside the United Kingdom.

Subsection (3) states that a statutory instrument containing an order in council under section 210,211,239,240,241 or 242 is subject to annulment in pursuance of a resolution of either House of Parliament.

Subsection (4) states that subsection (3) applies whether or not the order also contains other provisions made by Order in Council under-

the Foreign Marriage Act 1892 (c.23),

section 3 of the Foreign Marriage Act 1947 (c.33), or

section 39 of the Marriage Act 1949 (c.76).

Subsection (5) states that in sections 210,211,239,240 and 241 "prescribed" means prescribed by an Order in Council under the section in question.

Interpretation

Section 245 deals generally with interpretation. Subsection (1) of section 245 states that in this Part "United Kingdom national" means a person who is-

a) a British Citizen, a British overseas territories citizen, a British Overseas Citizen or a British National (overseas).
b) A British subject under the British Nationality Act 1981 (c.61) or
c) A British protected person, with the meaning of that Act.

Subsection (2) states that in this part "Her Majesty's forces" has the same meaning as in the Army Act 1955 (3&4 Eliz.2 C.18).

12

Relationships Arising Through Civil Partnerships

Part 6

Relationships arising through civil partnership

Interpretation of statutory references to stepchildren etc

Section 246 of the Civil Partnerships Act 2004 deals with interpretations of statutory references to stepchildren. Subsection (1) of section 246 states that in any provision to which this section applies, references to a stepchild or step-parent of a person (here "A") and cognate expressions, are to be read as follows-

A's stepchild includes a person who is the child of A's civil partner (but is not A's child);

A's step-parent includes a person who is the civil partner of A's parent (but is not A's parent);

A's stepdaughter includes a person who is the daughter of A's civil partner (but is not A's daughter);

A's stepson includes a person who is the son of A's civil partner (but is not A's son);

A's stepfather includes a person who is the civil partner of A's father (but is not A's parent);

A's stepmother includes a person who is the civil partner of A's mother (but is not A's parent);

A's stepbrother includes a person who is the son of the civil partner of A's parent (but who is not the son of either of A's parents);

A's stepsister includes a person who is the daughter of the civil partner of A's parent (but is not the daughter of either of A's parents).

Subsection (2) states that for the purposes of any provision to which this section applies-

"brother-in-law" includes civil partners brother;

"daughter-in-law includes civil partners daughter,

"father-in-law" includes civil partners father,

"mother-in-law" includes civil partners mother,

"parent-in-law includes civil partners parent,

"sister-in-law" includes civil partners sister, and

"son-in-law includes son's civil partner.

Provisions to which section 246 applies: Acts of Parliament etc

Section 247 deals with provisions to which section 246 applies. Subsection (1) of section 247 states that section 246 applies to-

a) any provision listed in Schedule 21 (references to stepchildren, in laws etc, in existing Acts),
b) except insofar as otherwise provided, any provision made by a future Act, and
c) except insofar as otherwise provided, any provision made by future subordinate legislation.

Subsection (2) states that a Minister of the Crown may, by order-

a) amend Schedule 21 by adding to it any provision of an existing Act,

b) provide for section 246 to apply to prescribed provisions of existing subordinate legislation.

Subsection (3) states that the power conferred by subsection (2) is also exercisable-

a) by the Scottish Ministers, in relation to a relevant Scottish provision,

b) by a Northern Ireland department, in relation to a provision which deals with a transferred matter;

c) by the National Assembly for Wales, if the order is made by virtue of subsection (2)(b) and deals with matters with respect to which functions are exercisable by the assembly.

Subsection (4) states that subject to subsection (5) the power to make an order under subsection (2) is exercisable by statutory instrument.

Subsection (5) states that any power of a Northern Ireland Department to make an order under subsection (2) is exercisable by statutory rule for the purposes of the Statutory Rules (Northern Ireland) Order 1979 (S.1 1979/1573 (N.I 12)).

Subsection (6) states that a statutory instrument containing an order under subsection (2) made by a Minister of the Crown is subject to annulment in pursuance of a resolution of either house of Parliament.

Subsection (7) states that a statutory instrument containing an order under subsection (2) made by the Scottish Ministers is subject to annulment in pursuance of a resolution of the Scottish Parliament.

Subsection (8) states that a statutory rule containing an order under subsection (2) made by a Northern Ireland department is subject to negative resolution (within the meaning of section 41 (6) of the Interpretation Act (Northern Ireland) 1954 (c.33 (N.I))).

Subsection (9) states that in this section-

"Act" includes an Act of the Scottish Parliament;

"existing Act" means an Act passed on or before the last day of the Session to which this Act is passed;

"existing subordinate legislation" means subordinate legislation made before the day on which this section comes into force;

"future Act" means an Act passed after the last day of the session to which this Act is passed;

"future subordinate legislation" means subordinate legislation made on or after the day on which this section comes into force;

"Minister of the Crown" has the same meaning as in the Ministers of the Crown Act 1975 (c.26);

"prescribed" means prescribed by the order;

"relevant Scottish provision" means a provision that would be within the legislative competence of the Scottish Parliament if it were include din an Act of that Parliament;

"subordinate legislation" has the same meaning as in the Interpretation Act 1978 (C.30) except that it includes an instrument made under an Act of the Scottish Parliament;

"transferred matter" has the meaning given by section (4)(1) of the Northern Ireland Act 1998 (c.47) and "deals with" in relation to a transferred matter is to be construed in accordance with section 98(2) and (3) of the 1998 Act.

Provisions to which section 246 applies: Northern Ireland

Section 248 deals with section 246 provisions in relation to Northern Ireland. Subsection (1) of section 248 states that sections 246 applies to-

a) any provision listed in Schedule 22 (references to stepchildren etc, in Northern Ireland legislation),
b) except insofar as otherwise provided, any provision made by any future Northern Ireland legislation, and
c) except insofar as otherwise provided, any provision made by any future subordinate legislation.

Subsection (2) states that the Department of Finance and personnel may by order-

a) amend Schedule 22 by adding to it any provision of existing Northern Ireland legislation;
b) provide for section 246 to apply to prescribed provisions of existing subordinate legislation.

Subsection (3) states that the power to make an order under subsection (2) is exercisable by statutory rule for the purposes of the Statutory Rules (Northern Ireland) Order 1979 (S.1 1979/1573 (N.I 12)).

Subsection (4) states that an order under subsection (2) is subject to negative resolution (within the meaning of section (41)(6) of the Interpretation Act (Northern Ireland) 1954 (1954 c.33 (N.I.))).

Subsection (5) states that in this section-

"existing Northern Ireland legislation" means Northern Ireland legislation passed or made on or before the last day of the Session in which this Act is passed;

"existing subordinate legislation" means subordinate legislation made before the day on which this section comes into force;

"future Northern Ireland legislation" means Northern Ireland legislation passed or made after the last day of the session in which this Act is passed;

"future subordinate legislation" means subordinate legislation made on or after the day on which this section comes into force;

"prescribed" means prescribed by the order;

"subordinate legislation" means any instrument (within the meaning of section (1)(c) of the Interpretation Act (Northern Ireland) 1954 c.33 (N.I.))).

13

Miscellaneous Provisions

Immigration control and formation of civil partnerships
Section 249 deals with immigration control and formation of civil partnerships. Schedule 23 of the CPA 2004 contains provisions relating to the formation of civil partnerships in the United Kingdom by persons subject to immigration control.

Gender recognition where applicant a civil partner
Section 250 deals with gender recognition. Subsection (1) of section 250 states that the Gender Recognition Act 2004 is amended as follows.

Subsection (2) states in-

a) section (3) (evidence) in subsection (6)(a), and
b) section (4) (successful applications) in subsections (2) and (3),

after "is married" insert "or a civil partner".

Subsection (3) states that in section (5) (subsequent issue of full certificates)-

a) in subsection (2), after "is again married" insert "or is a civil partner",
b) in subsection (6)(a) for "is not married" substitute "is neither married nor a civil partner", and
c) for the heading substitute "Issue of full certificates where applicant has been married".

Subsection (4) states that after subsection (5) insert-

"5A Issue of full certificates where applicant has been a civil partner

1) A court which-
a) makes final a nullity order on the ground that an interim gender recognition certificate has been issued to a civil partner, or
b) (in Scotland) grants a decree of dissolution on that ground,

must, on doing so, issue a full gender recognition certificate to that civil partner and send a copy to the Secretary of State.

2) If an interim gender recognition certificate has been issued to a person and either-
a) the persons civil partnership is dissolved or annulled (other wise than on the ground mentioned in subsection 91) in proceedings instituted during the period of 6 months beginning with the day on which it was issued, or
b) the persons civil partner dies within that period,

the person may make an application for a full gender recognition certificate at any time within specified in subsection (3) (unless the person again is a civil partner or married).

3) That period is the period of six months beginning with the day on which the civil partnership is dissolved or annulled or as the death occurs.
4) An application under subsection (2) must include evidence of the dissolution or annulment of the civil partnership and the date on which proceedings for it were

instituted, or of the death of the civil partner and the date on which it occurred.

5) An application under subsection (2) is to be determined by a Gender Recognition Panel.

6) The Panel-

a) must grant an application if satisfied that the applicant is neither a civil partner nor married, and

b) otherwise reject it.

7) If the Panel grants an application it must issue a full gender recognition certificate to the applicant.

Subsection (5) states that in-

a) section 7 (applications: supplementary), in subsection (1),

b) section 8 (appeals etc) in subsections (1) and (5), and

c) section 22 (prohibition on disclosure of information), in subsection (2)(a),

after "5 (2)" insert "5A(2)".

Subsection (6) states that in section 21 (foreign gender change and marriage, in subsection (4), after "entered into a later (valid) marriage" insert "or civil partnership".

Subsection (7) states that in section 25 (interpretation) in the definition "full gender recognition certificate" and "interim gender recognition certificate" for "or 5", 5 or 5A".

Subsection (8) states that in schedule 1 (Gender Recognition Panels) in paragraph 5, after "5(2)" insert 5A(2).

Subsection (9) states in Schedule 3 (registration) in paragraphs 9(1), 19(1) and 29(1) for"or5(2)" substitute ",5(2) or 5A(2).

Discrimination against civil partners in employment field

Section 251 deals with discrimination in employment. Subsection (1) of section 251 states that the Sex Discrimination Act 1975 (c.65) is amended as follows.

Subsection (2) states that for section 3 (discrimination against married persons in employment field) substitute-

"3 Discrimination against married persons and civil partners in employment field

(1) in any circumstances relevant for the purposes of any provision of Part 2, a person discriminates against a person ("A") who fulfils the condition in subsection (2) if-

a) on the ground of the fulfilment of the condition, he treats A less favourably than he treats or would treat a person who does not fulfil the condition, or

b) he applies to A a provision, criterion or practice which he applies or would apply equally to a person who does not fulfil the condition, but

i) which puts or would put persons fulfilling the condition at a particular advantage when compared with persons not fulfilling the condition, and

ii) which puts A at that disadvantage, and

iii) which he cannot show to be a proportionate means of achieving a legitimate aim.

2) The condition is that the person is-

a) married, or

b) a civil partner.

1) for the purposes of subsection (1) a provision of Part 2 framed with reference to discrimination against women is to be treated as applying equally to the treatment of men, and

for that purpose has effect with such modifications as are requisite"

Subsection (3) states that in section 5 (interpretation) for subsection (3) substitute-
"(3) Each of the following comparisons, that is-

a) a comparison of the cases pf persons of different sex under section 1(1) or (2),
b) a comparison of the cases of persons required for the purposes of section 2A, and
c) a comparison of the cases of persons who do and who do not fulfil the condition in section 3(2).

must be such that the relevant circumstances in the one case are the same, or not materially different, in the other.
Subsection (4) states that in section 7 (exception where sex is a genuine occupational qualification) in subsection (2) (h) for "by a married couple" substitute"-

i) by a married couple
ii) by a couple who are civil partners of each other, or
iii) by a married couple or a couple who are civil partners of each other".

Subsection (5) states that in section 65 (remedies on complaint under section 63) in subsection (1B) for "or marital status as the case may be" substitute "or (as the case may be) fulfilment of the condition in section 3(2)".

Discrimination against partners in employment field: Northern Ireland

Section 252 deals with Northern Ireland. Subsection (1) of section 252 states that the Sex Discrimination Act (Northern Ireland) Order 1976 (S.1 1976/1042 (N.I 15)) as follows.
Subsection (2) states that for Article 5 (discrimination against married persons in employment field) substitute-

"5 Discrimination against married persons and civil partners in employment field

1) In any circumstances relevant for the purposes of any provision of Part 3, a person discriminates against a person ("A") who fulfils the condition in paragraph (2) if-

a) on the ground of the fulfilment of the condition, he treats A less favourably than he treats or would treat a person who does not fulfil the condition, or

b) he applies to A a provision, criterion or practice which he applies or would apply equally to a person who does not fulfil the condition but-

    (i) which puts or would put persons fulfilling the condition at a particular disadvantage when compared with persons not fulfilling the condition

    (ii) which puts A at that disadvantage, and

    (iii) which he cannot show to be a proportionate means of achieving a legitimate aim

2) the condition is that the person is-

a) married, or

b) a civil partner.

3) For the purposes of paragraph (1), a provision of Part 3 framed with reference to discrimination against women is to be treated as applying equally to the treatment of men, and for that purpose has effect with such modifications as are requisite".

Subsection (3) states that for Article 7 (basis of comparison) substitute-

"7 Basis of comparison

Each of the following comparisons, that is-

a) a comparison of the cases of persons of different sex under Article 3(1) or (2),
b) a comparison of the cases of persons required for the purposes of Article 4A, and
c) a comparison of the cases of the persons who do and who do not fulfil the condition in Article 5(2),

must be such that the relevant circumstances in the one case are the same, or not materially different, in the other";

and omit Article 3(4).

Subsection (4) states in Article 10 (exception where sex is a genuine occupational qualification) in paragraph (2)(h) for " by a married couple" substitute-

(i)   by a married couple
(ii)   by a couple who are civil partners of each other, or
(iii)   by a married couple or a couple who are civil partners of each other.

Subsection (5) states that in Article 65 (remedies on complaint under Article 63), in paragraph (1B) for "or marital status as the case may be" substitute "or (as the case may be) fulfilment of the condition in Article 5 (2)".

Civil partners to have unlimited insurable interest in each other

Section 253 deals with insurance. Subsection (1) of section 253 states that where two people are civil partners, each of them is to be presumed for the purposes of section 1 of the Life assurance Act 1774 (c.48) to have an interest in the life of the other.

Subsection 92) states that for the purposes of section 3 of the 1774 Act, there is no limit on the value of the interest.

Social security, child support and tax credits

Section 254 deals with social security, child support and tax credit issues. Subsection (1) of section 254 states that Schedule 24 contains amendments relating to social security, child support and tax credits.

Subsection 92) states that subsection (3) applies in relation to any provision of any Act, Northern Ireland legislation or subordinate legislation which-

a) relates to social security, child support or tax credits and
b) contains references (however expressed) to persons who are living or have lived together as husband or wife.

Subsection (3) states that the power under section 259 to make orders amending enactments, Northern Ireland legislation and subordinate legislation is to be treated as including power to amend the provision to refer to persons who are living or have lived together as if they were civil partners.

Subsection (4) states that, subject to Subsection (5) section 175(3), (5) and (6) of the Social Security Contributions and Benefits Act 1992 (c.4) applies to the exercise of the power under section 259 in relation to social security, child support or tax credits as it applies to any power under that Act to make an order (there being disregarded for the purposes of this subsection the exceptions in section 175(3) and (5) of that Act).

Subsection (5) states that section 171(3), (5) and (6) of the Social Security Contributions and Benefits (Northern Ireland) Act 1992 (c.7) applies to the exercise by a Northern Ireland department of the power under section 259 in relation to social security and child support as it applies to any power under that Act to make an order (there being disregarded for the purposes of this subsection the exceptions in section 171(3) and (5) of that Act.

Subsection (6) states that the reference in subsection (2) to an Act or Northern Ireland legislation relating to social security is to be read as including a reference to-

a) the pneumoconiosis etc (Workers Compensation) Act 1979 (c.41), and
b) the pneumoconiosis etc, (Workers Compensation) (Northern Ireland) order 1979 (S.I 1979/925 (N.I.9));

and the references in subsection (4) and (5) to social security are to be construed accordingly.

Power to amend enactments relating to pensions

Section 255 contains power to amend enactments relating to pensions. Subsection (1) states that a Minister of the Crown may by order make such amendments, repeals or revocations in any enactment, Northern Ireland legislation, subordinate legislation or Church legislation relating to pensions, allowances or gratuities as he considers appropriate for the purpose of, or in connection with, making provision with respect to pensions, allowances or gratuities for the surviving civil partners or the dependants of deceased civil partners.

Subsection (2) states that the power conferred by subsection (1) is also exercisable-

a) by the Scottish Ministers, if the provision making the amendment, repeal or revocation is a relevant Scottish provision;
b) by a Northern Ireland department, if the provision making the amendment, repeal or revocation deals with a transferred matter.

Subsection (3) states that in the case of judicial pensions, allowances or gratuities, the power conferred by subsection (1) is exercisable-

a) in relation to any judicial office whose jurisdiction is exercised, exclusively in relation to Scotland, by the Secretary of State, or

b) subject to paragraph (a), by the Lord Chancellor.

Subsection (4) states that the provision which may be made by virtue of subsection (1)-

a) may be the same as, or different to, the provision made with respect to widows, widowers or the dependants of persons who are not civil partners, and

b) may be made with a view to ensuring that pensions. Allowances or gratuities take account of rights which accrued, service which occurred or any other circumstances which existed before the passing of this Act.

Subsection (5) states that the power conferred by subsection (1) is not restricted by any provision of this Act.

Subsection (6) states that before the appropriate person makes an order under subsection 91) he must consult such persons as he considers appropriate.

Subsection (7) states that subsection (6) does not apply-

a) to an order in the case of which the appropriate person considers that consultation is inexpedient because of urgency or

b) to an order made before the end of the period of 6 months beginning with the coming into force of this section.

Subsection (8) states that subject to subsection (9) the power to make an order under subsection (1) is exercisable by statutory instrument.

Subsection (9) states that any power of a Northern Ireland department to make an order under this section is exercisable by statutory rule for the purposes of the Statutory Rules (Northern Ireland) order 1979 (S.I. 1979/1573 (N.I 12)).

Subsection (10) states that an order under subsection (1) may not be made-

a) by a minister of the Crown, unless a draft of the statutory instrument containing the order has been laid before, and approved by a resolution of, each House of Parliament;
b) by the Scottish Ministers unless a draft of the statutory instrument containing the order has been laid before, and approved by a resolution of, the Scottish Parliament.
c) By a Northern Ireland department unless a draft of the statutory rule containing the order has been laid before, and approved by a resolution of, the Northern Ireland Assembly.

Subsection (11) states that in this section-

"the appropriate person" in relation to an order under this section, means the person making the order;

"Church legislation" means-

a) any measure of the Church Assembly or of the General Synod of the Church of England, or
b) any order, regulation or other instrument made under or by virtue of such a measure;

"enactment" includes an enactment comprised in an Act of the Scottish Parliament;
"Minister of the Crown" has the same meaning as in the Ministers of the Crown Act 1975 (c.26);
"relevant Scottish provision" means a provision that would be within the legislative competence of the Scottish Parliament if it were included in an Act of that Parliament;
"subordinate legislation" has the same meaning as in the Interpretation Act 1978 (c.30) except that it includes any instrument

made under an Act of the Scottish Parliament and any instrument within the meaning of section 1© of the Interpretation Act (Northern Ireland) 1954 (1954 c.33 (N.I)).

2transferred matter" has the meaning given by section 4(1) of the Northern Ireland Act 1998 (c.47) and "deals with" in relation to a transferred matter is to be construed in accordance with section 98(2) and (3) of the 1998 Act.

Amendment of certain enactments relating to pensions
Section 256 deals with amendments. Schedule 25 amends certain enactments relating to pensions

Amendments of certain enactments relating to the armed forces
Section 257 deals with the armed forces. Schedule 26 amends certain amendments relating to the armed forces.

Further information

For more information about civil partnerships, go to www.civilparnerships.org.uk

Or the Women and Equality unit website at www.equalitiesunit.gov.uk

Stonewall can provide information on www.stonewall.org.uk

Northern Ireland information on civil partnerships go to www.olmi.gov.uk

For information on civil partnership in Scotland go to www.scoltalnd.gov.uk/topics/Justice/civil/18313/12657

Tax-contact your local tax office or go to www.hmrc.gov.uk

Pensions-contact the pension service on 0845 6060265

Social security benefits-contact the benefit enquiry line on 0800 882200

Tax credits contact the tax Credits help line on 0845 3003900

Child Benefit- contact the child Benefit Help line on 08453021444 or e-mail child.benefit@hmrc.gsi.gov.uk

Child Support agency- contact 08457 133133

Adoption-for more information go to www.everchildmatters.gov.uk/socialcare/lookedafterchildren/adoption or contact your local council or voluntary adoption agency.

Immigration-contact the immigration and Nationality Bureau on 0870 667766 or go to www.ind.homeoffice.gov.uk

Relationship support – contact relate on 0300 100 1234

Domestic Violence – 0808 2000247 24 hour freephone

Broken Rainbow-LGTB domestic violence forum on 0300 999 5428.

INDEX

Appendix one

Facts and figures concerning civil partnerships from 2005-2010.

Number of civil partnership formations in the UK

YEAR	UK	ENGLAND	WALES	SCOTLAND	NI
2005	1,953	1,790	67	84	12
2006	16,106	14,383	560	1,047	116
2007	8,728	7,635	294	688	111
2008	7,169	6,276	282	525	86
2009	6,281	5,443	244	498	96

The above statistics show that, since 2005, the number of civil partnerships in all countries of the UK have diminished. The high point was one year after the legislation was enacted, 2006, where there was a very significant increase across the board. This reflected the fact that many same-sex couples in long standing relationships took advantage of the opportunity to formalise their relationship as soon as the legislation was implemented.

Civil partnerships by age and sex

In 2009, 51 per cent of civil partnerships formed in the UK were male compared with 53 per cent in 2008. The average age at formation of partnership for men in the UK fell from 41.8 years in 2008 to 41.2 years in 2009. For women this was 40.8 years in 2008 to 38.9 in 2009.

In 2009, as in previous years, London was the region in the UK with the highest number of registered civil partnerships. A quarter of all civil partnerships took place there. The areas with the largest number of civil partnership registrations in 2009 were:

- Westminster (182 male and 60 female civil partnerships)
- Brighton and Hove (123 male and 109 female)

Number of dissolutions

To obtain a civil partnership dissolution in the UK (see below), a couple must have been in either a registered civil partnership or a recognised foreign same-sex relationship for 12 months. There were 351 civil partnership dissolutions granted in the UK in 2009, compared with 180 in 2008 (a 95% increase). Of these 327 were in England and Wales, 24 in Scotland and none in Northern Ireland. There were more women than men dissolving a civil partnership in England, Wales and Scotland. See table below.

YEAR	UK	ENGLAND AND WALES	SCOTLAND	NI
2007	41	40	1	0
2008	180	166	14	0
2009	351	327	24	0

The above table shows the steadily increasing number of dissolutions.

Dissolutions by age, sex and previous legal partnership

Over 50% of civil partners obtaining a dissolution in the UK in 2009 were aged between 35 and 49 years whereas only 13per cent were aged 50 or over. The figures for the UK show that a greater proportion of males civil partnership dissolutions were in the higher age group than females. Eighteen per cent of male civil partners dissolving a partnership were aged 50 years and over compared with only 10 per cent of females.

The average age at dissolution of partnership for men in the UK increased from 39.1 years in 2008 to 39.9 years in 2009 and from 37.4 years to 38.7 years for women.

In 2009, 15 per cent of men and 21 per cent of women dissolving a civil partnership in the UK had been in a previous marriage or civil partnership.

Source: Office for National Statistics

List of Schedules to the Civil Partnerships Act 2004

To access the following Schedules go to the government website mentioned at beginning of book.

Schedule 1. Prohibited degrees of relationship: England and Wales

Part 1. The prohibitions

Schedule 2. Civil partnerships of persons under 18: England and Wales.

Part 1. Appropriate persons.
Part 2. Obtaining consent: general
Part 3. Obtaining consent: special procedure
Part 4. Provisions relating to the court

Schedule 3. Registration by former spouses one of whom has changed sex.

Schedule 4. Wills, administration of estates and family provisions.

Part 1. Wills
Part 2. Administration of estates and family provisions

Schedule 5. Financial relief in the county court or High Court etc.

Part 1. Financial relief in connection with dissolution, nullity or separation.
Part 2. Property adjustment on or after dissolution, nullity or separation.
Part 3. Sale of property orders.
Part 4. Pension sharing orders on or after dissolution or nullity order.

Part 1. Amendments of the Family Law Act 1996 (c.27).

Part 2. Consequential amendments.

Part 3. Transitional provisions.

Schedule 10. Forbidden degrees of relationship (Scotland)

Schedule 11. Financial provisions in Scotland after Overseas proceedings.

Part 1. Introductory.

Part 2. Circumstances in which court may entertain Application for final provision.

Part 3. Disposal of application.

Part 4. The expression "order for financial provision".

Schedule 12. Prohibited degrees of relationship Northern Ireland.

Schedule 13. Civil partnerships of persons under 18 Northern Ireland.

Part 1. Appropriate persons.

Part 2. Dispensing with courts.

Part 3. Recording consents and orders.

Schedule 14 Wills, administration of estates and family provisions etc.

Part 1. Wills

Part 2. Administration of estates family provisions.

Schedule 15. Financial relief in the High Court, county court etc Northern Ireland.

Part 1. Financial provision in connection with dissolution, nullity or separation.

146

Part 2. Property adjustment on or after dissolution, nullity or separation.

Part 3. Pension sharing orders on or after dissolution or nullity orders.

Part 4. Matters to which court is to have regard under parts 1-3.

Part 5. Making of part 1 orders having regards to pension benefits.

Part 6. Pension protection fund compensation etc.

Part 7. Maintenance pending outcome of dissolution, nullity or separation proceedings.

Part 8. Failure to maintain financial provision (and interim orders)

Part 9. Commencement of certain proceedings, and duration of certain orders.

Part 10. Variation, discharge etc of certain orders for financial relief.

Part 11. Arrears and repayments.

Part 12. Consent orders and maintenance agreements.

Part 13. Miscellaneous and supplementary.

Schedule 16. Financial relief in court of summary jurisdiction etc. Northern Ireland.

Part1. Failure to maintain etc. Financial provision.

Part 2. Orders for agreed financial provision.

Part 3. Orders of court where civil partners living apart by agreement.

Part 4. Interim orders.

Part 5. Commencement and duration orders under parts 1-3

Part 6. Variation etc of orders.

Part 7. Arrears and repayments.

Part 8. Supplementary.

Schedule 17. Financial relief in Northern Ireland after overseas dissolution etc of a civil partnership.

Part 1. Financial relief

Part 2. Steps to prevent avoidance prior to application for relief under paragraph 4.

Schedule 18. Housing and tenancies Northern Ireland.

Schedule 19. Family homes and domestic violence in Northern Ireland.

Part 1. Amendments of the Family Homes and Domestic Violence (Northern Ireland) Order S1 1998/1071 (N16)).

Part 2. Consequential amendments.

Part 3. Transitional provisions.

Schedule 20. Meaning of overseas relationships: specified relationships.

Schedule 21. References to stepchildren etc in existing Acts.

Schedule 22. References to stepchildren etc in existing Northern Ireland legislation.

Schedule 23. Immigration control and formation of civil partnerships.

Part 1. Introduction.

Part 2. England and Wales

Part 3. Scotland.

Part 4. Northern Ireland.

*Part 5.*Regulations.

Schedule 24. Social security, child support and tax credits.

Part 1. Amendments of the Child Support Act 1991 (c.48).

Part 2. Amendments of the Child Support Act (Northern Ireland) order 1991.

Part 3. Amendments of Social Security Contributions and Benefits Act 1992.

Part 4. Amendments of the Social Security Administration Act (Northern Ireland) 1992 (c.5).

Part 5. Amendment of the Social Security Contributions and Benefits Act 1992 (c.7).

Part 6. Amendments of the Social Security and Administration Act (Northern Ireland) Act 1992 (c.8).

Part 7. Amendment of the Jobseekers Act 1995 (c.18).

Part 8. Amendments of the Child Support Act 1995 (c.34)

Part 9. Amendments of the Child Support (Northern Ireland) Order 1995.

Part 10. Amendments of the Job Seekers Order (Northern Ireland) 1995.

Part 11. Amendments of the Social Security Act 1998.

Part 12. Amendments of the Social Security (Northern Ireland) Order 1998.

Part 13. Amendments of the State Pensions Credit Act 2002.

Part 14. Amendment of the Tax Credit Act 2002 (c.2).

Part 15. Amendment of the State Pensions Credits Act (Northern Ireland) 2002.

Schedule 25. Amendments of certain enactments relating to pensions.

Schedule 26. Amendments of certain enactments relating to armed forces.

Schedule 27. Minor and consequential amendments.

Schedule 28. Consequential amendments Scotland.

Part 1. Amendments of the Succession (Scotland) Act 1964 (c.41).

149

Part 2. Amendments of the Family Law (Scotland) Act 1985, (c.37).

Part 3. Amendments of the bankruptcy (Scotland) Act 1985.

Part 4. Miscellaneous amendments.

Schedule 29. Minor and consequential amendments (Northern Ireland).

Schedule 30. Repeals and revocations.

Emerald Publishing
www.emeraldpublishing.co.uk

Brighton BN7 2SH

Other titles in the Emerald Series:

Law
Guide to Bankruptcy
Conducting Your Own Court case
Guide to Consumer law
Creating a Will
Guide to Family Law
Guide to Employment Law
Guide to European Union Law
Guide to Health and Safety Law
Guide to Criminal Law
Guide to Landlord and Tenant Law
Guide to the English Legal System
Guide to Housing Law
Guide to Marriage and Divorce
Guide to The Civil Partnerships Act
Guide to The Law of Contract
The Path to Justice
You and Your Legal Rights

Health
Guide to Combating Child Obesity
Asthma Begins at Home

Music
How to Survive and Succeed in the Music Industry

General
A Practical Guide to Obtaining probate
A Practical Guide to Residential Conveyancing
Writing The Perfect CV
Keeping Books and Accounts-A Small Business Guide

Business Start Up-A Guide for New Business
Finding Asperger Syndrome in the Family-A Book of Answers
Explaining Autism Spectrum Disorder
Explaining Alzheimers and Dementia

For details of the above titles published by Emerald go to:

www.emeraldpublishing.co.uk